SECRET INGREDIENT
SMOKING AND GRILLING

SECRET INGREDIENT

STACI JETT
Winner of Travel Channel's
American Grilled

INGREDIENT

SMOKING AND GRILLING

INCREDIBLE RECIPES FROM A COMPETITIVE CHEF TO TAKE YOUR BBQ TO THE NEXT LEVEL

PAGE STREET
PUBLISHING CO.

PAGE STREET
PUBLISHING CO.

First published in 2017 by
Page Street Publishing Co.
27 Congress Street, Suite 105
Salem, MA 01970
www.pagestreetpublishing.com

Distributed by Macmillan, sales in Canada by The Canadian Manda Group.

21 20 19 18 17   1 2 3 4 5

ISBN-13: 978-1-62414-389-2
ISBN-10: 1-62414-389-X

Library of Congress Control Number: 2016917975

Cover and book design by Page Street Publishing Co.
Photography by Ken Goodman

Printed and bound in the United States

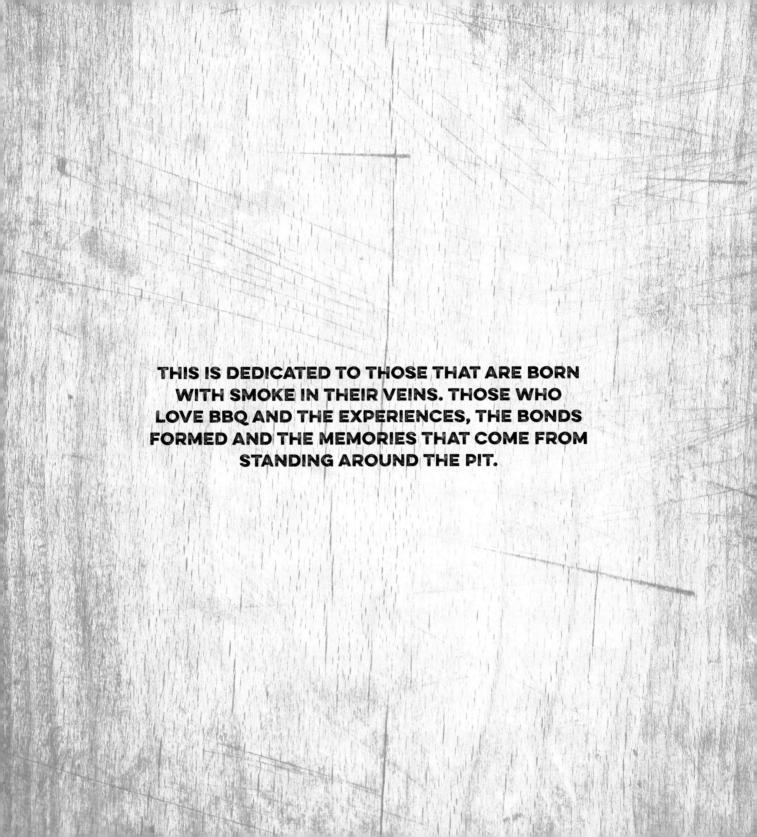

THIS IS DEDICATED TO THOSE THAT ARE BORN WITH SMOKE IN THEIR VEINS. THOSE WHO LOVE BBQ AND THE EXPERIENCES, THE BONDS FORMED AND THE MEMORIES THAT COME FROM STANDING AROUND THE PIT.

{ CONTENTS }

FOREWORD

#BBQLIFE

This hashtag is meaningful to many of us who love to fire it up—from restaurant owners, to folks who team up and enter every cook-off they can find, to the ones who love to burn wood in their backyards on the weekends. We all share this passion, and social media feeds the addiction and brings this barbecue community together.

The Internet has brought so many great cooks to our attention over the years. One in particular who caught my eye was a little lady from Kentucky. It was as if everything she touched was magic. Her award-winning barbecue, inventive dessert entries, catering services and game-processing skills all come together as the Staci Jett package. I have always been amazed at what she can come up with.

But who is Staci Jett? To me she will always be "Miss Staci." She's a mom, a butcher, an entrepreneur, a pitmaster, a farmer, a daddy's girl and so much more. She gives her all to every challenge she decides to take on. She works hard, plays hard and loves hard. Staci is one of the people I will always appreciate.

She has won awards in multiple barbecue contests and she was a finalist on *Chopped*. After that, she won *American Grilled*. I know how hard it must have been not to tell me the results before it aired. I wanted to wait for the airing and I'm so glad I did. It was fun watching her pull that win.

Not too many people have impressed the barbecue world like she has. Her extensive smoking and grilling knowledge and her unique flavor combinations make her stand out in the crowd. I am so proud of the way she has made things happen for herself. I know that the best is yet to come.

Her favorite line from Shakespeare fits her so well, "And though she be but little, she is fierce." That she is.

Enjoy Miss Staci's first book. These recipes are game-changers and I know you are going to love them!

–ANDREW "DREW SMOKE" LEEPER
Columnist for *The BBQ Times*

INTRODUCTION

I was lucky enough to have a terrific childhood. I grew up in the country, where I could play outside, run barefoot, make mud pies, catch lightning bugs and play with the critters. My dad and mom both worked and my babysitter and best friend was my grandma.

I was very fortunate to have Grandma in my life. She fixed supper for my parents every evening and she raised a garden every year. She was a great country cook. She put love into everything she prepared. All her dishes were from scratch. Nothing was measured. It was a touch of this and a dash of that. There were corn cakes or biscuits at every meal, some sort of meat and several sides. We drank sweet tea and said our blessing before we ate.

I would watch Grandma bake and cook and help where I could. As I got older, I took over preparing the nightly meal. She was still there by my side and cleaning the dishes up behind me as I went. You know, they say a messy cook is a good cook. Well, I was as messy as it got.

My dad was the griller in the family. I was quite small but still remember him building a brick grill in the backyard. I thought it was something else to watch him grill hot dogs, hamburgers and the occasional steak. That old brick grill is where Dad would cook country hams in an old lard pot. They took hours to cook and were the best thing since sliced bread. The old brick grill is gone now, but it gave birth to my love of grilling. To grill brings back so many memories and feelings of joy.

I have always been competitive. So, marrying that competitive nature and love for cooking started me down the road that I am on today. I started in backyard cook-offs for charity and then became a pro on the barbecue competition circuit.

Being Southern and country, I tend to have a big personality crammed into a small stature. I'm not afraid to dream big and go for my dreams, either. So, one day I threw my hat in the ring and decided to audition for my first television cooking show. I was in shock when I got the call to be on. Then and there I was bit by the bug. I went on to win that grilling show and later appeared on another. I never thought it was possible for someone from such a small town to go that far.

SECRET INGREDIENT SMOKING AND GRILLING

Since then I have won several more awards for my grilling experience, which has taken me to the World Food Championships. And that's how this book has come to be—all from cooking at my grandma's knee to grilling hot dogs with my dad. It's all a part of what makes me "me."

In this book, I showcase what I do best: barbecue. I decided to take it up a notch and give you my secrets to standout backyard cooking. Each recipe has my secret weapon that you won't see coming. Some use a pinch of special spice; some feature a kind of meat you wouldn't expect. No matter the recipe, you're going to end up with an impressive dish you'll want to make over and over again.

This book is filled with recipes that are full of memories and creations that I just have a liking for. I hope that you enjoy it—and make some delicious barbecue along the way.

Staci Jett

BORDERLINE SINFUL BEEF AND BISON

"THE STORY OF BARBECUE IS THE STORY OF AMERICA: SETTLERS ARRIVE ON GREAT UNSPOILED CONTINENT, DISCOVER WONDROUS RICHES, SET THEM ON FIRE AND EAT THEM."

–VINCE STATEN

Beef and bison have roamed the American countryside for centuries. Bison were once hunted on the open ranges and farmers raised cattle as a source of meat, milk and butter. Now, bison numbers in the wild are way down, but they are farmed on ranches to provide consumers with a constant supply of meat. Once thought of as a high-end meat, bison can now be found in many chain grocers. Whereas farmers and cooks pride our beef for its fat content, we also praise the bison for its lack thereof. Bison is a great alternative for those on restricted diets. I don't worry about calories when it involves a superb cut of meat off the grill, though there have been a few steaks in my life that were responsible for a food coma or two. Give me beef or bison in any form. Light that fire and light your imagination.

KENTUCKY BEER-BRAISED BEEF SHORT RIBS

Here, the beer adds richness and the fresh herbs add depth of flavor. Even if you don't think you like cooking with beer, I can assure you this recipe will change your mind. This recipe pairs perfectly with my Roasted Turnip and Yukon Gold Mashed Potatoes (page 114).

SERVES: 8

SHORT RIBS

4 lb (1.8 kg) prime beef short ribs

Chop House Seasoning

1 cup (160 g) diced sweet onion

½ cup (60 g) diced carrot

½ cup (55 g) diced celery

4 cloves garlic, minced

8 rosemary sprigs

8 stems fresh thyme

4 bay leaves

1 cup (235 ml) Kentucky Bourbon Barrel Ale

3 cups (705 ml) beef stock

1 tbsp (18 g) kosher salt

1 tbsp (6 g) fresh black pepper

ONION RINGS

Canola oil, for frying

1 cup (235 ml) Kentucky Bourbon Barrel Ale

2 cups (260 g) cornstarch

1 tbsp (6 g) Creole seasoning

1 sweet onion, sliced into rings

GRAVY

Pan drippings

Beef stock

1 tbsp (8 g) cornstarch

To make the short ribs, coat the ribs generously with the seasoning. Let the ribs rest for an hour.

Preheat the grill to 375°F (190°C). Preheat a smoker to 275°F (140°C), using oak and cherry wood.

Sear the ribs on the grill for a couple of minutes on each side. Transfer the ribs to the smoker and smoke for 2 hours.

Transfer the ribs to an aluminum pan, add the diced onion, carrot, celery, garlic, rosemary, thyme, bay leaves, beer and beef stock. Sprinkle with the kosher salt and black pepper. Cover the pan with foil and return it to the smoker for another 2½ hours or until tender. The cook time depends on the thickness of the ribs.

(continued)

KENTUCKY BEER-BRAISED BEEF SHORT RIBS (CONT.)

To make the onion rings, heat 1 inch (2.5 cm) of oil in a heavy skillet to 375°F (190°C). Pour the beer into a bowl and combine the cornstarch and Creole seasoning on a shallow plate, stirring to blend well. Dip the onion rings into the beer and then dredge in the seasoned cornstarch. Fry until crispy, about 1 minute. Remove with a spider or slotted spoon and drain on a paper towel–lined plate. Set them aside until you are ready to assemble the dish.

To make the gravy, remove the ribs from the pan and strain the pan drippings through a fine-mesh strainer. Skim off the fat and add the drippings to a saucepan. If needed, add enough beef stock to equal 2 cups (470 ml). Heat the mixture over medium heat until it comes to a boil. In a small bowl, stir the cornstarch into ¼ cup (60 ml) cold beef stock and whisk into the saucepan. Continue to whisk until the mixture has thickened. Lower the heat and keep the gravy warm.

To serve the beef ribs, I like to lay down a bed of my potato and turnip mash, place a rib in the center of the mash, drizzle the rib with the gravy and top with onion rings. Mmm mmm, good eating right there.

TRIPLE B WAGYU PRETZEL BURGERS

Wagyu beef is the highest quality beef in the United States. It is often compared to the Kobe beef of Japan, but Wagyu is a cross of Angus and Kobe. This beef is prized for its extreme marbling of fat, and this richness makes it difficult to eat a large portion. Burgers made from Wagyu should be handled as a fine steak and cooked to a perfect medium. This may be a complex burger with several components, but you've never had a burger this delicious in your life.

SERVES: 3

BURGERS

1 lb (454 g) Wagyu ground beef

3 tbsp (18 g) Chop House Seasoning

6 thick slices bacon

3 pretzel buns

1 cup (20 g) arugula

SWEET BUTTER SPREAD

4 tbsp (56 g) unsalted sweet cream butter

4 cloves roasted garlic (see Note)

Kosher salt and black pepper to taste

SWEET BOURBON GLAZE

½ cup (120 ml) Devil's Cut bourbon

1 cup (225 g) packed light brown sugar

1 tbsp (10 g) minced sweet onion

2 tbsp (28 g) unsalted sweet cream butter

⅓ cup (80 ml) water

1 tbsp (15 ml) red wine vinegar

1 tbsp (15 ml) Worcestershire sauce

1 tsp (5 ml) Tiger Sauce

¼ tsp kosher salt

¼ tsp ground black pepper

BEER CHEESE SAUCE

½ cup (60 g) diced chipotle Gouda cheese

1 (5-oz [140-g]) jar Kraft Old English Cheese Spread

3 oz (84 g) Alouette sharp cheddar

6 tbsp (90 ml) Kentucky Bourbon Barrel Ale

2 tsp (10 g) Grey Poupon Country Dijon mustard

2 tsp (10 g) creamy horseradish

¼ tsp chipotle powder

HORSERADISH MAYO

1 tsp (3 g) creamy horseradish

¼ cup (60 g) mayonnaise

FRIED SWEET ONION AND JALAPEÑO RINGS

Canola oil, for frying

1 large sweet onion, sliced into thin rings

3 fresh jalapeños, sliced into rings

1 cup (235 ml) Kentucky Bourbon Barrel Ale

3 cups (360 g) cornstarch

(continued)

TRIPLE B WAGYU PRETZEL BURGERS (CONT.)

Preheat the grill to 375°F (190°C).

To make the burgers, let the beef sit at room temperature for 10 minutes. Letting the meat come up to temperature allows it to cook more evenly. Divide the beef into 3 portions and form each into a patty. Coat each well with 1 tablespoon (6 g) of the Chop House Seasoning.

Cook the bacon on the grill until it becomes crispy. Place the burgers on the grill and cook until medium, about 4 minutes per side, or until the center reaches 150°F (65°C) on a meat thermometer.

To make the butter spread, mix all of the ingredients together in a small bowl. Spread the butter on the tops and bottoms of the buns and place them butter-side-down on the grill for 2 minutes.

To make the bourbon glaze, mix all of the ingredients in a small skillet and simmer over medium heat until the glaze reduces by half. Keep warm.

To make the beer cheese, mix all ingredients in a saucepan over low heat, whisking occasionally until creamy. Keep the sauce warm until you are ready to assemble the burgers.

To make the horseradish mayo, stir together the horseradish and mayonnaise in a small bowl.

Finally, to make the onion and jalapeño rings, heat 1 inch (2.5 cm) of oil in a heavy skillet to 375°F (190°C). Pour the beer into a bowl and spread the cornstarch on a shallow plate. Dip the onion and jalapeño rings into the beer and then dredge in the cornstarch. Fry until crispy, about 1 minute. Remove with a spider or slotted spoon and drain on a paper towel–lined plate. Set them aside until you are ready to assemble the dish.

To assemble the burgers, spread the horseradish mayo on the bottom bun and top each with 2 slices of the bacon, a burger, a spoonful of beer cheese and the onion and jalapeño rings. Next, drizzle with 1 teaspoon (5 g) of the bourbon sauce and top with the arugula.

NOTE: If you can't find roasted garlic in your local grocery, making it is simple. I take a whole bulb of garlic and slice the top off to expose the cloves. Place the bulb in foil with a sprinkle of oil and salt. Seal the foil and bake/smoke in a 275°F (135°C) oven until the garlic is soft and golden, 25 to 30 minutes. Squeeze the cloves out of their skins.

STEAKHOUSE BURGERS

This burger is like having a surf and turf dinner at a famous steak house, with beef, crab and creamy Brie all on a brioche bun. The secret to this burger's success is the creamy, spreadable Brie and the crab. The cheese can make or break a burger. So, if you haven't tried this cheese before, make an effort to find it. Who needs to go out to eat? Stay home and be your own five-star chef tonight.

SERVES: 2

1 lb (454 g) ground sirloin

1 tbsp (6 g) Montreal Steak Seasoning

1 tbsp (15 ml) A.1. Steak Sauce

⅓ cup (40 g) lump crabmeat

1 tbsp (15 ml) remoulade sauce

⅓ cup (40 g) blanched asparagus tips

1 tsp (3 g) diced red bell pepper

2 brioche hamburger buns

2 tbsp (20 g) Alouette Crème de Brie

Arugula

Preheat the grill to 375°F (190°C).

In a medium-size bowl, combine the sirloin, Montreal Steak Seasoning and A.1. Steak Sauce until well blended. Divide the meat into 2 portions and form each into a large patty. Let sit at room temperature for 10 minutes. Letting the meat come up to temperature allows it to cook more evenly.

In another bowl, combine the crabmeat, remoulade sauce, asparagus tips and red bell pepper. Cover the mixture and keep refrigerated until the burgers are done and ready to assemble.

Place the burgers on the grill and cook for 5 minutes on each side, or until the center reaches 150°F (65°C) on a meat thermometer. Remove the burgers from the grill.

Toast the buns and spread 1 tablespoon (10 g) of the Brie on the bottom of each bun. Top with a burger, a handful of arugula and half of the crab mixture and replace the top hamburger bun. Cook one of these for your sweetie and you'll be a star.

SPICY CHEESE-STUFFED MEATBALL HOAGIES

I am a meat and taters girl. I worship the beef gods, to say the least. What goes with ground beef? Bacon and cheese, please. I love this big, manly sandwich. The secret is the pocket of melty cheese waiting to be discovered in the center of this devilish bacon meatball. This oh so flavorful, juicy creation and the crusty toasted bread will satisfy your biggest hunger. So, man up, put your big girl panties on and dig in with both hands.

SERVES: 4

MEATBALLS

½ lb (227 g) ground chuck

½ lb (227 g) ground bacon

½ lb (227 g) ground veal

2 large eggs

2 tsp (7 g) chopped garlic

¼ cup (4 g) chopped flat-leaf parsley

¼ cup (30 g) plain bread crumbs

¼ tsp onion powder

½ tsp kosher salt

¼ tsp ground black pepper

2 jalapeños, finely chopped

1 (8-oz [227-g]) block Kraft Pepper Jack cheese, cubed

RUB

1 cup (225 g) packed light brown sugar

½ tsp onion powder

1 tsp (2 g) Old Bay Seasoning

2 tbsp (12 g) smoked paprika

1 tsp (2 g) chipotle powder

½ tsp kosher salt

½ tsp chili powder

½ tsp ancho chile powder

½ tsp garlic powder

BARBECUE SAUCE

1 cup (235 ml) Sweet Baby Ray's Honey Chipotle Barbecue Sauce

⅓ cup (80 ml) Frank's RedHot Sweet Chili Sauce

¼ cup (60 ml) Tiger Sauce

HOAGIES

4 hoagie rolls, toasted

20 dill pickle slices

¾ cup (120 g) sliced sweet onion

Prepare your grill for two-zone cooking. If you are using a charcoal grill, burn the charcoal on only one side of your grill. If you have a gas grill, only light one side of your burners. Preheat the grill to 300°F (150°C). I like to add a couple of applewood chunks and a couple of Jack Daniel's Bourbon Barrel Chunks for flavor and smoke.

To make the meatballs, combine all the ingredients except for the cheese cubes in a large bowl. I like to use my hands to mix well; it helps to incorporate the ingredients better. Next, take enough of the meat mixture to form a ball the size of a golf ball. Take a cube of the cheese and press it into the center of each meatball. Form the meat around the cheese to completely hide the cube. You should have around 20 meatballs.

To make the rub, combine all of the ingredients in a bowl. Lightly coat the meatballs with a dusting of the rub. Place the meatballs on the grill over indirect heat. Smoke these beauties for 30 minutes.

Meanwhile, to make the barbecue sauce, combine all of the ingredients in a saucepan. Bring the sauce to a simmer and lower the heat to keep warm. Toss the meatballs in the sauce to coat them.

Place your meatballs on the toasted hoagie rolls and top with the pickles and onion. *Shew wee!* That's good eatin'.

BISON PHILLY-STUFFED BELL PEPPERS

I love stuffed peppers and Philly cheesesteaks. I ran across this recipe prepared with deli roast beef. Oh, heck no. My secret? I want meat, real meat. Make sure these are served hot right off the grill. If you still crave the bread portion of the cheesesteak, just serve up a nice crusty baguette alongside. I know it's not how the purest eat a cheesesteak, but this recipe sure will make you question all you thought you knew about a Philly.

SERVES: 2

2 bison strip steaks

1 tbsp (6 g) Longhorn Steakhouse Grill Seasoning

2 green bell peppers

1 shallot, thinly sliced

4 slices provolone cheese

Prepare your grill for two-zone cooking. If you are using a charcoal grill, light half a chimney starter with lump charcoal. Let it burn until all of the coals show some white ash. Pour the charcoal to only one side of your grill. If you have a gas grill, only light one side of your burners.

Season the bison steaks with the grill seasoning. Let sit at room temperature for 10 minutes. Letting the meat come up to temperature allows it to cook more evenly. Place the steaks over direct heat and sear for 4 minutes per side. Remove them from the grill and let them rest for 10 minutes.

Slice the bell peppers in half lengthwise and clean out the seeds and white membranes. Place the peppers in the microwave and heat them for 1 to 2 minutes, depending on your microwave's wattage. Place the pepper halves in a baking dish. Thinly slice the steaks and fill the peppers with the steak and the sliced shallot. Top each pepper with a slice of provolone cheese. Place the dish back on the grill over indirect heat for 5 minutes. Pull the peppers from the grill and dig in.

SMOKED MEATLOAF

It's funny, the memories that slip into your mind sometimes when you don't realize it. My meatloaf has always been very simple. For some reason, it was always my grandma's favorite. If she went to a potluck she would ask me to prepare one for her to take. When she returned, she would be all smiles from the compliments received. The secret ingredient is the salsa. Why spend time dicing peppers, onions and tomatoes when the salsa has that covered for you?

SERVES: 4–6

---

1 lb (454 g) ground chuck

½ lb (227 g) ground pork

½ lb (227 g) ground veal

1 cup (240 g) Pace Thick and Chunky Salsa

1 tsp (6 g) kosher salt

¾ cup (90 g) Quaker quick oats

2 eggs

1 cup (240 g) ketchup

½ tsp chili powder

3 tbsp (35 g) diced bell pepper

Preheat the smoker to 250°F (120°C).

Combine the chuck, pork, veal, salsa, salt, oats and eggs in a large bowl. Form into a loaf and place the meatloaf in a baking dish. Place in the smoker and cook for 1½ hours, or until the internal temperature reaches 160°F (71°C) on a meat thermometer.

Combine the ketchup and chili powder in a small bowl. Brush the glaze on the entire meatloaf about 10 minutes before it is done. Finish the meatloaf by sprinkling the diced bell pepper over the top. I like to serve this with mashed taters and mac and cheese.

POOR MAN'S COUNTRY HAMBURGER STEAK

I have some recipes included in my book that are quite long and take some effort, and I have some that are very simple and fast to prepare. This would have to be one of the fastest, but it delivers a warm, home-cooked meal fit for a king or queen on a busy weeknight. Anything covered in gravy is a hit with my family. The Chop House Seasoning makes the burger taste like a fine steak. It can be purchased online and is a must-have to make this dish special. Just make sure you have plenty of bread to sop it all up.

SERVES: 4–6

2 lb (908 g) ground chuck

4 tbsp (40 g) Chop House Seasoning

1 large sweet onion, thinly sliced

1 (1-lb [454-g]) package sliced button mushrooms

GRAVY

2 cups (470 ml) beef stock

¼ tsp black pepper

½ tsp kosher salt

1 tsp (3 g) chopped garlic

2 tsp (16 g) cornstarch

1 tsp (5 ml) Worcestershire sauce

½ tsp chopped fresh thyme

½ tsp ground coriander

Preheat the grill to 275°F (135°C).

Divide the ground chuck into 4 to 6 portions and form into patties. Season the burgers with the Chop House Seasoning and let sit at room temperature for 10 minutes. Letting the meat come up to temperature allows it to cook more evenly. Grill them for 5 minutes per side, or until the center reaches 150°F (65°C) on a meat thermometer. Transfer the burgers from the heat to a large cast-iron skillet or pan. Cover the burgers with the sliced onion and mushrooms.

To make the gravy, whisk together the stock, pepper, salt, garlic, cornstarch, Worcestershire, thyme and coriander in a bowl. Pour the mixture over the burgers. Cover the pan and place it back on the grill for 20 to 25 minutes, or until the gravy thickens. If this is poor man's food, then please take all of my money.

BEEF SUMMER SAUSAGE

I processed deer and livestock for locals for more than ten years in my own meat room on my farm. Being a butcher is something that you must love and take pride in. It is a dying skill and is even more rare for women to do. I loved the stories told by the hunters as they dropped off their deer, and I loved the pride in the farmer's voice as he spoke about his prize hog or steer. One of my services was making summer sausage and jerky. I was asked quite often for my recipe. I would just chuckle and say, "Well, if I told you, then you wouldn't need me." The cat is now out of the bag. The secret ingredient is the Morton Sugar Cure without the seasoning packet. This is my basic recipe, but it can be customized thousands of ways. For example, if you like it spicy, then add hot peppers and cheese. I recommend rough-chopping block cheese such as cheddar or Pepper Jack. You can also purchase high-temperature cheeses online that won't melt into the meat as much.

MAKES: one 3-lb (1.3-kg) roll

---

3 lb (1362 g) ground beef

1 tbsp (6 g) Montreal Steak Seasoning

1 tbsp (10 g) Morton Sugar Cure without the seasoning packet added

1 summer sausage casing

In a large bowl, combine the beef, seasoning and sugar cure and mix together very well. Let the meat cure in the refrigerator for a couple of hours. Once the meat has set up, you can run it through a stuffer into a summer sausage casing. Wet the casings in warm water for 2 minutes. Feed the mixture into the stuffer and fill the casings until the meat is 1½ to 2 inches (3.8 to 5 cm) from the top. Twist the top of the casing and tie with butcher string.

Preheat a smoker to 225°F (100°C) with hickory and cherry wood.

Smoke for 2½ hours. The casings will be tight and the sausage will be firm but not hard. Let cool and wrap in plastic wrap or in a zip-top bag and store in the fridge. If you do not wrap it, it will dry out like hard salami. I had some people tell me they would slice it thick and fry some up for breakfast.

PRIME RIB ROAST

I was raised with the notion that when there was an occasion to celebrate, we all got together to eat a meal. Same still stands true to today. When some big life event pops up, such as a birthday, a birth or a marriage, we still celebrate with food. To me there is nothing better than a big ol' rib eye. I once said, "Take me out and buy me something off of the dollar menu at McDonald's, or buy me a $50 steak dinner." That's the key to my heart. Smoking with Jim Beam Oak Barrel Smoking Chips is my secret technique to add that caramel oak flavor to the meat.

SERVES: 14

1 (7-lb [3.2-kg]) rib roast

Dale's Seasoning

Montreal Steak Seasoning

Rub the outside of the roast with the Dale's Seasoning and then coat it generously with the Montreal Steak Seasoning. Do not be afraid to use a good bit of seasoning. Remember, this is a big piece of meat. Wrap the roast up tight in plastic wrap and chill in the fridge overnight.

The next day, preheat your smoker to 275°F (135°C) using Jim Beam Oak Barrel Smoking Chips and cherry wood.

Remove the roast from the refrigerator and let sit at room temperature for at least 20 minutes. Letting the meat come up to temperature allows it to cook more evenly. Add the roast to the smoker and use a probe to keep an eye on the internal temperature. It's very important to do this low and slow so the ends aren't well done. After 4 hours, check the temperature of the center of the roast. Pull it out of the smoker to rest once the probe reaches 140°F (60°C).

Allow the roast to rest for at least 10 minutes so the juices won't run when it's cut. Some folks like to get fancy by coating the rib roast with fresh herbs and horseradish sauce before they smoke it. I say save the horseradish sauce to serve alongside as a condiment. That way, you won't have to worry about that one person who isn't a fan of a good steak/horseradish combo.

*See photo on page 35.

BISON SHEPHERD'S PIE

Shepherd's pie is traditionally made using lamb mixed with vegetables and a mashed potato topping, hence the name. In the United States most people know it as having a beef filling. But either way you serve it, this pie is known as a poor man's supper. By incorporating the bison, wine and a few special ingredients, I'm taking this dish to an elevated level.

SERVES: 4–6

---

3 lb (1.4 kg) ground bison

1 tbsp (6 g) Hungarian sweet paprika

1½ tsp (9 g) kosher salt

1 tsp (2 g) ground black pepper

2 tbsp (30 ml) olive oil

1 cup (160 g) chopped sweet onion

½ cup (60 g) peeled chopped carrot

½ cup (55 g) chopped celery

3 cloves garlic, chopped

1 cup (235 ml) dry red wine

2 cups (470 ml) beef stock

1 cup (180 g) diced fire-roasted tomatoes

1 tsp (1 g) chopped fresh thyme

1 cup (130 g) frozen peas

2 cups (150 g) peeled and diced turnips

⅓ cup (40 g) all-purpose flour

1 recipe Roasted Turnip and Yukon Gold Mashed Potatoes (page 114)

Preheat the smoker to 300°F (150°C).

In a large Dutch oven over medium heat, brown the ground bison with the paprika, salt, pepper, olive oil, onion, carrot, celery and garlic, about 10 minutes, or until the pink is gone. Add the wine, beef stock, tomatoes, thyme, peas, turnips and flour. Mix well, cover the pot with the lid, place in the smoker and cook for 1½ hours, until the turnips are tender and the mixture has thickened.

Remove the pot from the smoker, spread the mashed potatoes on the top of the bison filling, making sure it reaches the edges, and place it back, uncovered, into the smoker for another 20 minutes. Cool for 15 minutes before serving.

COFFEE-RUBBED BISON TENDERLOIN WITH HORSERADISH HENRY BAIN SAUCE

My first run-in with bison was when I competed on *American Grilled*. I was given this huge bison tenderloin as a secret ingredient. I had never tasted one or broken one down before. Thank goodness as a butcher I knew to treat it as I would beef. The secret to the rub is the addition of the coffee. Coffee makes the meat pop with beefy goodness. Henry Bain sauce is another recipe with Kentucky roots. It can be found in some stores and online. It was so good that it won me the title of Louisville Grillmaster and the crew cleaned up the leftovers fast.

SERVES: 4

HORSERADISH HENRY BAIN SAUCE

1 cup (250 g) mango chutney

1 cup (240 g) ketchup

½ cup (120 ml) A.1. Steak Sauce

¼ cup (60 ml) Worcestershire sauce

1½ cups (360 g) chili sauce

1 tbsp (10 g) grated fresh horseradish

TENDERLOIN

1 cup (225 g) packed brown sugar

1 tbsp (6 g) instant coffee

½ tsp salt

½ tsp black pepper

1 tsp (2 g) Old Bay Seasoning

½ tsp onion powder

½ tsp chili powder

1 (2-lb [908-g]) bison tenderloin

To make the sauce, combine all of the ingredients in a blender and process until smooth. Transfer the sauce to a bowl, cover and refrigerate overnight.

Prepare your grill for two-zone cooking. If you are using a charcoal grill, burn the charcoal on only one side of your grill. If you have a gas grill, only light one side of your burners. Preheat the grill to 300°F (150°C).

To make the tenderloin, combine the brown sugar, coffee, salt, pepper, Old Bay, onion powder and chili powder in a bowl. Coat the bison with the rub. Let sit at room temperature for 10 minutes. Letting the meat come up to temperature allows it to cook more evenly.

Place the tenderloin over indirect heat and grill for 20 minutes. Move the tenderloin over to direct heat and sear until the internal temperature reaches 145°F (63°C) on a meat thermometer. Keep a close eye on the bison because the sugars in the rub can easily burn. Remove the bison from the grill and let it rest for 10 minutes. Cut it into thin slices and serve with the Horseradish Henry Bain Sauce.

BISON STRIP STEAK WITH ARUGULA PESTO

Bison is becoming as available in grocery stores as beef is. My local Kroger store started carrying it in the form of strip steaks, rib eye, stew meat and ground meat. It is a lean, healthy meat that doesn't have a gamey flavor. Just like any good steak, the secret is to let the meat come to room temperature before grilling. This will allow the steak to cook evenly by bringing it closer to its final eating temperature. The peppery arugula pesto complements the meat better than any steak sauce ever could. Please do me and your steak a favor and don't grill the poor thing 'til it's well done. There is no greater crime than taking a piece of meat and turning it into shoe leather. It will lose so much flavor and become tough and dry.

SERVES: 2

---

2 bison strip steaks

2 tbsp (30 ml) Moore's Marinade

1 tbsp (6 g) Longhorn Steakhouse Grill Seasoning

ARUGULA PESTO

2 cups (40 g) arugula

½ cup (50 g) grated Parmesan cheese

¼ cup (32 g) toasted pine nuts

2 cloves garlic

Juice of ½ lemon

Pinch of kosher salt

½ cup (120 ml) extra virgin olive oil

Preheat your grill to 300°F (150°C).

Rub the steaks with the Moore's Marinade. Let sit at room temperature for 10 minutes. Letting the meat come up to temperature allows it to cook more evenly.

To make the arugula pesto, place the arugula, Parmesan, pine nuts, garlic, lemon juice and salt in a food processor and process until the mixture is well blended and crumbly. With the processor running, slowly drizzle in the olive oil through the feed tube until the pesto thickens and becomes creamy.

Sprinkle the grill seasoning on each steak right before placing them on the grill. Cook for 4 minutes on each side, or until the center reaches 140°F (60°C). Remove from the heat and allow them to rest for 5 minutes before serving. Drizzle the pesto on top of each steak and serve.

FREAKISHLY GOOD CHICKEN AND OTHER FEATHERED FOWL

"IF YOU REALLY WANT TO MAKE A FRIEND, GO TO SOMEONE'S HOUSE AND EAT WITH HIM . . . THE PEOPLE WHO GIVE YOU THEIR FOOD GIVE YOU THEIR HEART."

—CESAR CHAVEZ

There is nothing better than a finger-licking fried chicken dinner. However, the grill and smoker are some awesome tools to expand your menu options. Don't be afraid to try different spices or even ingredients you may have never heard of. Each recipe contains spices or ingredients that turn an everyday dish into a star. When smoking poultry, it is best to play around with fruit woods and a touch of hickory. Cherry always imparts beautiful color and smoke to any protein. Grilling gives it that char and caramelization that take flavors over the top. There is no right or wrong when it comes to being creative. You never know—maybe one day you could be the next Colonel Sanders.

SWEET CHILI SMOKED WINGS

When most people think of wings, they think of drummies and flats. Not me. I like to keep my wings whole. I believe it's the satisfaction of using both hands to experience the taste, touch and pure euphoria of the chicken wing. It allows more sauce to stick in each tasty crevice. This is one of my favorite recipes for wings. The herby and smoky rub works very well to complement the sweetness of the Frank's RedHot Sweet Chili Sauce. The sweet with a touch of heat will definitely have you licking your fingers and wanting more.

SERVES: 4

RUB

1 cup (200 g) turbinado sugar

½ tsp kosher salt

2 tbsp (12 g) Weber Kick'n Chicken Seasoning

1 tsp (2 g) Old Bay Seasoning

¼ tsp onion powder

1 tsp (2 g) chili powder

¼ cup (24 g) paprika

½ tsp chipotle powder

½ tsp ground coriander

24 whole chicken wings

2 (12-oz [355-ml]) bottles Frank's RedHot Sweet Chili Sauce

⅓ cup (5 g) chopped fresh cilantro, for garnish

⅓ cup (45 g) chopped cashews, for garnish

To make the rub, combine all of the rub ingredients in a food processor and blend until smooth.

Place the chicken wings in a large zip-top bag along with the rub. Toss the wings until they are completely coated. Place in the fridge or cooler for at least 4 hours or up to overnight. The longer the wings set, the better the penetration of the rub into the meat.

Prepare your grill for two-zone cooking. If you are using a charcoal grill, burn the charcoal on only one side of your grill. If you have a gas grill, only light one side of your burners. Preheat the grill or smoker to 250°F (120°C). I smoke my wings with Royal Oak Chef Select charcoal, cherry and hickory wood chunks. The hickory gives the wings that light smoke flavor while the cherry adds a great color and light cherry undertones.

Smoke the wings for 45 minutes over indirect heat, then transfer them to direct heat and grill the wings, turning them often so they don't burn. The wings are done when the internal temperature reaches 165°F (74°C) on a meat thermometer. Remove them from the heat and toss them in the sweet chili sauce. Finish with a sprinkle of fresh cilantro and cashews.

CHICKEN POT PIE

Most folks grew up with memories of their mom popping those little store-bought pot pies into the oven on a cool weeknight for supper. At the time, we thought there could be nothing better. Ah, but there is. The secret here is to smoke the chicken as well as the pot pie itself. Smoking the pot pie adds a depth of flavor that regular baking cannot compete with. The Montreal Chicken Seasoning contains herbs and spices that will fill the air with the smell of fall and memories of home. Sorry, Mom, we still love you.

SERVES: 4–6

1 (4- to 5-lb [1.8- to 2.3-kg]) whole chicken

1 tsp (2 g) McCormick Montreal Chicken Seasoning, plus extra to coat the chicken

2 tsp (6 g) chopped garlic

1 cup (120 g) sliced carrot

1 cup (150 g) frozen green peas

½ cup (55 g) sliced celery

⅓ cup (75 g) unsalted butter

⅓ cup (53 g) chopped sweet onion

⅓ cup (40 g) all-purpose flour

¼ tsp salt

¼ tsp black pepper

1¾ cups (411 ml) chicken stock

⅔ cup (160 ml) milk

2 (9" [23-cm]) unbaked pie crusts

Prepare your grill for two-zone cooking. If you are using a charcoal grill, burn the charcoal on only one side of your grill. If you have a gas grill, only light one side of your burners. Preheat the grill or smoker to 300°F (150°C). Soak cherry and hickory pieces in water, then drain and add on top of the coals in the grill or smoker.

Season the outside and inside cavity of the chicken with the Montreal Chicken Seasoning. Place the chicken in the smoker or over indirect heat on the grill and cook for 1 to 1½ hours, depending on the size of the chicken. Test for doneness by inserting a thermometer into the thigh; you want a temperature of 165°F (74°C). Remove the chicken from the heat and let it rest for 10 minutes. This allows time for the juices to redistribute into the chicken. If you carve the chicken immediately after removing it from the heat the juices will run out, resulting in dry chicken. Carve the meat off of the chicken and dice the meat into chunks.

In a large bowl, combine 2½ cups (350 g) of the chicken and the garlic, carrots, peas and celery.

In a saucepan over medium heat, cook the butter and onions until they are soft and translucent, about 5 minutes. Stir in the flour, salt, pepper and Montreal Chicken Seasoning. Slowly stir in the stock along with the milk. Simmer over medium-low heat for about 5 minutes, or until the mixture thickens. Remove it from the heat and stir in the chicken and vegetable mixture.

Fit one of the pie crusts into a pie plate and spread the chicken filling on the bottom. Cover the top with the other pie crust and seal by pressing the edges of the crust together with the tines of a fork. Cut several slits in the top of the pie to allow the steam to escape.

Cook the pie in the smoker for 20 to 30 minutes, or until the pastry is golden brown and the filling is bubbly. Cool for at least 10 minutes before serving.

BUFFALO CHICKEN CHILI

What on earth could be better than combining the flavor of a Frank's RedHot Buffalo chicken wing and a good hearty bowl of chili? I have entered several charity chili cook-offs with this recipe and it has won over and over with great reviews. This isn't your run-of-the-mill chili. The secret is to add bleu cheese to your bowl before you devour it. Say good-bye to the ordinary. This chili and a cold beer will certainly be the hit at your next football tailgate.

SERVES: 8

1 (4- to 5-lb [1.8- to 2.3-kg]) whole chicken

Tony Chachere's Creole Seasoning

2 tbsp (28 g) unsalted butter

1 large carrot, peeled and finely chopped

1 large sweet onion, chopped

3 stalks celery, chopped

3 tbsp (30 g) chopped garlic

5 tbsp (30 g) chili powder

2 tbsp (12 g) ground cumin

1 tbsp (6 g) paprika

¾ cup (180 ml) Frank's RedHot Buffalo Sauce

2 (15-oz [420-g]) cans tomato sauce

1 (15-oz [420-g]) can fire-roasted tomatoes

1 (15-oz [420-g]) can navy beans

1 (19-oz [532-g]) can red kidney beans

4 cups (940 ml) chicken stock

Salt and pepper to taste

Bleu cheese crumbles, for garnish

Preheat your smoker to 300°F (150°C) using apple and hickory woods.

Season the outside and inside cavity of the chicken with the Creole seasoning. It is important to season the inside cavity because the seasoning penetrates the meat from all angles. Smoke the chicken for 1 to 1½ hours depending on the size of the chicken. Test for doneness by inserting a thermometer into the thigh; you want a temperature of 165°F (74°C). Remove the chicken from the heat and let it rest for 10 minutes. Remove the skin from the chicken and pull the chicken into bite-size pieces.

In a large stockpot, combine the chicken, butter, carrot, onion, celery, garlic, chili powder, paprika, Buffalo sauce, tomato sauce, tomatoes, beans and stock. Cover the pot with a lid and simmer the chili over medium-low heat for an hour, until the veggies are tender and the flavors have blended. Season to taste with salt and pepper. Garnish with bleu cheese crumbles. Just like any soup or chili, this one is even better the next day.

MEDITERRANEAN GRILLED CHICKEN WRAP

I am a sucker for Mediterranean flavors. Olives, white wine and feta cheese make me one happy girl. Grilled chicken is one of my favorite dishes, but it can become boring. So, combining these two loves seemed like the right thing to do. Boy, was I right. The secret here is definitely the marinade. If you have the time, let the chicken bathe in the flavors as long as possible.

SERVES: 4

---

4 boneless skinless chicken breasts

2 tbsp (30 g) Mezzetta Olive, Parmesan & Garlic Everything Spread

2 tbsp (30 ml) white wine

2 tbsp (30 ml) olive oil

½ tsp Greek seasoning

4 pita wraps

4 tbsp (40 g) crumbled feta cheese

8 slices tomato

Sliced red onion

Shredded romaine lettuce

⅓ cup (80 g) mayonnaise

Juice of ½ lemon

Salt and pepper to taste

In a zip-top bag, combine the chicken breasts, spread, wine, olive oil and Greek seasoning. Massage the chicken until it is fully coated with the marinade, and then place the chicken in the fridge to marinate for 4 hours.

Prepare your grill for two-zone cooking. If you are using a charcoal grill, burn the charcoal on only one side of your grill. If you have a gas grill, only light one side of your burners. Preheat the grill to 275°F (135°C).

Remove the chicken from the bag, place it on the grill over indirect heat and let it cook for about 10 minutes. Move the chicken over direct heat to finish cooking, about 10 more minutes. The chicken is done when it reaches 165°F (74°C) on a meat thermometer. Pull the chicken off the heat and allow it to rest for 10 minutes before slicing it into thin slices.

Assemble the sandwich by placing 1 sliced breast on each wrap. Top the chicken with 1 tablespoon (10 g) of the feta, 2 slices of tomato, red onion slices and shredded lettuce. In a small bowl, stir together the mayonnaise and lemon juice and a sprinkle of salt and pepper. Drizzle the mayo mixture over the filling. So tasty you will wonder how you ever got by with plain grilled chicken.

HAWAIIAN CHICKEN

This recipe was born after a client asked for a grilled chicken dish but wanted something more exciting than just plain grilled or barbecued chicken. Fruit pairs very well with chicken, and the addition of melty cheese and smoky ham only tantalize the taste buds even more. The secret here is to grill the pineapple to add a caramel dimension to the flavor. This recipe can be dressed up for dinner or eaten on a bun. Either way, you can't go wrong.

SERVES: 4

---

4 boneless skinless chicken breasts

1 cup (235 ml) Wish-Bone Fat Free Italian Dressing

1 tbsp (6 g) Weber Kick'n Chicken Seasoning

4 slices Swiss cheese

8 slices smoked ham

4 pineapple rings

⅓ cup (80 ml) Paula Deen Sweet Bourbon Glaze, plus more for serving

Place chicken and dressing in a zip-top bag and marinate in the fridge for at least 4 hours.

Prepare your grill for two-zone cooking. If you are using a charcoal grill, burn the charcoal on only one side of your grill. If you have a gas grill, only light one side of your burners. Preheat your grill to 275°F (135°C).

Place the chicken breasts over indirect heat and sprinkle them with the chicken seasoning. Cook the breasts for 10 minutes and then move them over to direct heat to grill for another 10 minutes, or until the internal temperature reaches 165°F (74°C) on a meat thermometer. Set the chicken in a shallow baking dish and top each piece with 1 slice of cheese and 2 slices of ham. Grill the pineapple over direct heat for a couple of minutes on each side, and then place 1 ring on top of each chicken breast. Drizzle the bourbon glaze over all and return the pan to indirect heat for a couple of minutes to melt the cheese. Serve warm with extra sauce.

CHICKEN DUMPLINGS

It seems that every family has its own version of chicken and dumplings. To me, it is a thick and creamy chicken base with oodles of tender chicken and veggies. In most recipes, the chicken is either roasted and added to the pot or simmered in the broth whole and then chopped. My recipe adds a depth of flavor by slow smoking the whole chicken first and then pulling the meat. Another secret is to use the cheap biscuits and never use biscuits with layers. The cheap biscuits hold together and will not become gooey or slimy. The cream of chicken soup adds creaminess and richness to round out the dish.

SERVES: 6–8

---

1 (4- to 5-lb [1.8- to 2.3-kg]) whole chicken

McCormick Montreal Chicken Seasoning

6 cups (1.4 L) chicken stock

2 stalks celery, chopped

2 cups (240 g) diced baby carrots

1 sweet onion, diced

1 (10.5-oz [294-g]) can Campbell's Cream of Chicken Soup

4 (7.5-oz [210-g]) cans Pillsbury Buttermilk Biscuits

2 tbsp (12 g) Montreal Steak Seasoning

Preheat the smoker to 275°F (135°C).

Rub the outside and the inside cavity of the chicken with the chicken seasoning. Place the chicken in the smoker and cook for 1½ hours, or until a thermometer inserted into the thigh reaches 165°F (74°C). Remove the chicken from the smoker. Remove the skin from the chicken and discard. Carve the meat off of the chicken and set it aside until it is ready to go into the pot.

In a large stockpot, combine the chicken stock, celery, carrots, onion, soup and the diced chicken. Bring the mixture to a simmer over medium heat. Roll out the biscuits one at a time and slice them into strips. Drop the strips into the liquid, stirring after each addition of a few biscuits. Repeat until all of the biscuits are in the pot. Season with the Montreal steak seasoning and simmer until thickened.

SOUTHWESTERN STUFFED PEPPERS

I don't know of anyone in the barbecue world who doesn't have their own recipe for stuffed jalapeños wrapped in bacon (also known as ABT, or atomic buffalo turds). Well, those who know me know that I dance to my own beat, so of course mine are a tad different. The secret is to use mini sweet peppers instead of jalapeños. They add a sweet flavor that works with the chicken, while the element of heat comes from the chipotle powder and the jalapeño in the filling. You may notice that I have an affection for Montreal Chicken Seasoning. The spices work well to complement many meats and veggies. See what ya think.

SERVES: 4–6

---

1 tbsp (6 g) Montreal Chicken Seasoning

1 tbsp (15 ml) olive oil

3 boneless skinless chicken breasts

1 (15-oz [420-g]) can black beans, drained and rinsed

1 (1-lb [454-g]) bag frozen sweet corn

1 jalapeño, diced

½ tsp ground cumin

½ tsp chipotle powder

2 cups (240 g) shredded Monterey Jack cheese

1 (1-lb [454-g]) bag mixed mini sweet peppers

Prepare your grill for two-zone cooking. If you are using a charcoal grill, burn the charcoal on only one side of your grill. If you have a gas grill, only light one side of your burners. Preheat the grill to 275°F (135°C).

Combine the chicken seasoning and olive oil in a small bowl and rub over the chicken breasts. Grill the breasts over indirect heat for 10 minutes, then move the chicken to direct heat and grill for another 10 minutes, turning a couple of times. Remove the chicken and allow it to rest for 5 minutes before chopping it into a fine dice.

In a large bowl, combine the beans, corn, jalapeño, cumin, chipotle powder and cheese. Carefully stir in the chopped chicken. Cut each pepper in half lengthwise and remove the seeds. Fill the peppers with the chicken mixture, place them in a baking dish and return to the grill over indirect heat. Cook for 10 minutes, or until the cheese is melted and the tops start to turn golden.

PROSCIUTTO-WRAPPED STUFFED TURKEY BREAST

I am a huge fan of slow-roasted comfort foods—ones that take all day and make the house smell so good and inviting. Turkey always makes me think of cozy blankets and blazing fires. Nothing warms my heart more than the smell of turkey filled with the goodness of gooey cheese and topped with my secret weapon, salty prosciutto.

SERVES: 6–8

---

1 (4-lb [1.8-kg]) turkey breast

1 tbsp (6 g) poultry seasoning

½ tsp kosher salt

2 tsp (10 ml) olive oil

⅓ cup (50 g) chopped shallot

2 cloves garlic, minced

1¾ cups (245 g) diced butternut squash

½ cup (72 g) Craisins

1 cup (30 g) spinach

3 sage leaves, chopped

¼ cup (38 g) chopped pecans

1 (8-oz [227-g]) package prosciutto

Preheat the smoker to 275°F (135°C).

Slice the turkey breast so it opens and lies flat. Place the turkey between two pieces of wax paper and pound until it is about 1 inch (2.5 cm) thick. Sprinkle the poultry seasoning all over the outside of the turkey and let it rest while you prepare the filling.

In a heavy skillet over medium heat, combine the salt, oil, shallot, garlic and squash. Sauté for 8 to 10 minutes, then add the Craisins, spinach, sage and pecans. Cook for a few more minutes, until the squash is tender. Remove the filling from the heat and allow it to cool.

Spread the cooled stuffing on the inside of the turkey breast. Roll the turkey up and cover the outside with the prosciutto. Tie the roll with butcher's string. Smoke the stuffed turkey breast for an hour and then check the internal temperature. Once the turkey reaches 165°F (74°C) it is ready to come off. The outside will be golden and crisp. Let the turkey rest for 15 minutes before slicing.

KENTUCKY HOT BROWN TURKEY BURGER

One of the best-known turkey dishes comes from Louisville and the Brown Hotel. The Kentucky Hot Brown consists of a thick slice of bread, sliced turkey, bacon, tomato and a creamy cheese sauce. This burger is a play on that famous dish. I created it for a competition in which you created a dish the represented your state. It won me a golden ticket to the World Food Championships. I even threw in my secret weapon, a beer cheese made with Kentucky Ale. Even if you don't think you are a fan of turkey burgers, this one may change your mind.

SERVES: 2

BURGERS

2 tbsp (16 g) minced sun-dried tomato

½ cup (80 g) diced sweet onion

3 tbsp (45 ml) olive oil

1 tsp (6 g) kosher salt

½ tsp coarsely ground black pepper

2 fresh sage leaves, chopped

2 sprigs rosemary, leaves stripped and chopped

4 thyme sprigs, chopped

½ tsp Weber Kick'n Chicken Seasoning

2 cloves garlic, minced

1 lb (454 g) Honeysuckle White ground turkey

KENTUCKY ALE WHITE BEER CHEESE

1 (3.95-oz [111-g]) package Sargento Tastings Aged Vermont White Cheddar, cubed

⅓ cup (35 g) grated Parmesan

8 oz (227 g) Velveeta Queso Blanco, cubed

½ tsp McCormick Montreal Steak Seasoning

¾ cup (180 ml) Kentucky Ale

¼ tsp creamy horseradish

FIXIN'S

2 large pretzel buns

6 slices Roma tomato

4 slices thick-cut pepper bacon, cooked

4 leaves red leaf lettuce

(continued)

KENTUCKY HOT BROWN TURKEY BURGER (CONT.)

Preheat the grill to (300°F [150°C]).

To make the burgers, combine the sun-dried tomato, onion, oil, salt, pepper, sage, rosemary, thyme and seasoning in a small skillet over medium heat. Sauté until the onions are soft, about 5 minutes. Add the garlic and continue to sauté for 2 more minutes. Remove the skillet from the heat. Let the mixture cool completely and then combine it with the ground turkey. Form the turkey into 2 large patties. Cover the patties with plastic wrap and place them in the fridge for at least 30 minutes to let the flavors mingle.

To make the beer cheese, combine all the ingredients in a small saucepan over medium heat and cook, whisking, until the cheese is melted and creamy. Lower the heat to keep the cheese warm while the burgers are cooking.

Remove the burgers from the refrigerator and let sit at room temperature for 10 minutes. Place the burgers on the grill and cook on each side for 6 minutes, or until a thermometer inserted into the center reaches 165°F (74°C). Remove the burgers from the heat and let them rest for 5 minutes before assembling the burger.

To assemble the fixin's, place the buns on the grill to toast the cut sides. Remove from the heat and top with a patty, 2 tablespoons (30 ml) of the beer cheese, 3 slices of tomato, 2 slices of bacon and 2 lettuce leaves. Serve the extra beer cheese on the side.

BEER-MARINATED CORNISH HEN WITH STONE-GROUND MUSTARD KENTUCKY ALE SAUCE

I may be a bourbon girl, but there is one drink that I enjoy just as much, and that's my Kentucky Bourbon Barrel Ale. This dish is a twist on beer can chicken. The rich oak flavor from the beer combined with the stone-ground mustard makes the recipe a winner. The secret ingredient is most certainly the stone-ground mustard. With each bite of the succulent hen you get a pop from the mustard seeds—a taste bud euphoria.

SERVES: 2

---

2 (1- to 2-lb [454- to 908-g]) Cornish game hens

4 tbsp (40 g) McCormick Montreal Chicken Seasoning

1 (12-oz [355-ml]) bottle Kentucky Bourbon Barrel Ale

½ cup (115 g) packed dark brown sugar

Juice from 1 lime

4 tbsp (40 g) minced red onion

1 head of garlic, chopped

2 tsp (10 ml) olive oil

1 tbsp (6 g) minced fresh ginger

MUSTARD ALE SAUCE

½ cup (120 ml) Kentucky Bourbon Barrel Ale

2 tbsp (22 g) stone-ground mustard

1 shallot, finely chopped

½ tsp black pepper

3 cups (705 ml) chicken stock

¼ cup (60 ml) heavy cream

Place the hens in a zip-top bag with the bottle of ale, brown sugar, lime juice, onion, garlic, olive oil and ginger. Let the hens marinate in the fridge for 8 hours or up to overnight.

Season the hens inside and out with the Montreal Chicken Seasoning.

Preheat the smoker or grill to 275°F (135°C).

Smoke the hens for 1 hour, or until a meat thermometer inserted into the thigh reaches 165°F (74°C). Let the hens rest while you prepare the mustard ale sauce.

To make the sauce, bring the ale, mustard, shallot and pepper to a boil in a medium saucepan. Simmer until the mixture is reduced by half, 5 to 10 minutes. Add the chicken stock and reduce the sauce down to 2 cups (470 ml), about 25 minutes. Add the cream and simmer until the sauce coats the back of a spoon, about 6 minutes. Serve the hens with the sauce spooned over the top.

GRILLED DUCK BREAST WITH CRANBERRY ORANGE SAUCE AND SWEET POTATO HASH

Duck is a dark, rich meat that is perfect for the grill. Pairing it with tart flavors, such as cranberry and orange, helps cut the richness from the fat. Getting the skin to crisp is the secret to great duck. Using McCormick Grill Mates Brown Sugar Bourbon Seasoning on the duck complements the earthiness of the smoked sweet potatoes. Taking the extra steps, such as smoking the potatoes, is what creates a special dish like this one.

SERVES: 2

---

2 (1-lb [454-g]) duck breasts

1 tbsp (15 ml) olive oil

2 tsp (4 g) McCormick Grill Mates Brown Sugar Bourbon Seasoning

SWEET POTATO HASH

2 sweet potatoes

3 slices bacon

½ cup (80 g) diced sweet onion

2 cloves garlic, minced

1 tsp (1 g) chopped fresh rosemary

⅓ cup (45 g) Craisins

¼ cup (35 g) chopped pecans

CRANBERRY ORANGE SAUCE

1 (12-oz [340-g]) bag fresh cranberries

¼ cup (60 ml) water or white wine

¾ cup (180 g) Smucker's orange marmalade

¾ cup (150 g) sugar

¼ tsp ground cinnamon

Preheat the smoker to 275°F (135°C).

Score the skin on the duck breasts and rub the breasts with the olive oil and bourbon seasoning. Place the duck in the refrigerator to marinate while you prepare the sweet potato hash and the cranberry orange sauce.

To make the hash, wrap the sweet potatoes in foil and cook them in the smoker for 1 hour. This will help break down the potato and add flavor from the smoke. Remove the potatoes and let rest until cool enough to handle. Peel the skin and cube the sweet potatoes. Fry the bacon in a large skillet over medium heat until crisp, about 5 minutes, then remove it from the skillet. Pour off all but 2 tablespoons (30 ml) of the bacon grease. Add the potatoes and onion to the skillet and crumble the bacon in. Let the potatoes cook over medium heat, stirring every few minutes for about 6 minutes. Next, add the garlic, rosemary, Craisins and pecans. Cook the hash for 6 minutes longer, stirring every few minutes, or until the potatoes are tender.

Meanwhile, to make the sauce, add the cranberries, wine, marmalade and sugar to a heavy-bottomed saucepan. Cover and cook over medium heat, stirring frequently, until the cranberries break down. If the mixture becomes too thick, add a little more wine. Use a potato masher or fork to help break up the cranberries. Keep the hash and cranberry sauce warm while the duck grills.

Preheat your grill to 275°F (135°C). Grill the duck breasts, skin side down, for 5 minutes. Be careful to watch the grill for flare-ups. Flip the duck over to do a quick sear. The duck is done when a thermometer inserted into the thickest part of the breast reaches 145°F (63°C). Remove the duck and let it rest for 5 minutes before slicing. Serve the duck over the hash with a drizzle of the cranberry orange sauce on top.

NOT YOUR MOMMA'S PORK AND LAMB

"LEARN HOW TO COOK, TRY NEW RECIPES, LEARN FROM YOUR MISTAKES, BE FEARLESS AND ABOVE ALL HAVE FUN!"

—JULIA CHILD

There are so many possibilities when it comes to pork and lamb. They are both very mild meats that have endless possibilities for flavors and seasonings. I know that we sometimes fall into a rut of cooking the same dishes over and over, but where is the fun in that? I think Julia hit the nail on the head. So instead of buying the breakfast sausage in the tube at the grocery store, experiment with making your own at home. Don't worry about making a mistake: Think of it as an opportunity to learn and broaden your culinary horizons.

BARBECUED PORK TENDERLOIN PIZZA

There are just some things in life that are worth the effort and the calories. I must confess this might be one of them. I wanted to simplify the recipe so anyone could recreate this at home, so I chose tenderloins because they cook faster. If you have the time to smoke your own pork shoulder, even better. Naan bread makes the perfect crust with its light texture. The secret is mixing the blackberry jam with the barbecue sauce. It gives a depth of flavor that you don't get using the barbecue sauce on its own. Make a couple of these pies at home because they will disappear fast.

SERVES: 4–6

⅓ cup (67 g) Sugar In The Raw

1 tsp (2 g) Old Bay Seasoning

1 tbsp (6 g) smoked paprika

½ tsp chili powder

¼ tsp salt

¼ tsp garlic powder

¼ tsp onion powder

1 (1-lb [454-g]) pork tenderloin

½ cup (112 g) unsalted butter, softened

1 tbsp (10 g) minced roasted garlic

2 Stonefire naan breads

4 cups (480 g) Italian blend shredded cheese

½ red onion, thinly sliced

1 cup (235 ml) Sweet Baby Ray's Honey Chipotle Barbecue Sauce

1 tbsp (14 g) Smucker's seedless blackberry jam

In a small bowl, combine the sugar, Old Bay, paprika, chili powder, salt, garlic powder and onion powder and stir to blend. Use this as your rub for the tenderloin. Let the pork marinate in the fridge for at least 4 hours.

Preheat your smoker to 250°F (120°C).

Smoke the tenderloin for 1 hour, or until it reaches 145°F (63°C) on a meat thermometer. Pull the pork from the smoker and let it cool. The pork will need to be sliced very thin. Make sure you have a sharp knife for this task.

Prepare your grill for two-zone cooking. If you are using a charcoal grill, burn the charcoal on only one side of your grill. If you have a gas grill, only light one side of your burners. Preheat the grill to 275°F (135°C).

In a small bowl, combine the butter and roasted garlic. Spread the butter mixture on the bread. Divide the tenderloin slices, cheese and sliced onion between the two pizzas. Place the pizzas over indirect heat for 10 minutes, or until the cheese is melted and turning golden around the edges. While the pizzas are on the grill, mix the barbecue sauce and the jam in a small bowl and heat in the microwave for a minute. Stir and heat for up to a minute more, or until the jam has dissolved. Drizzle the barbecue sauce over the tops of the baked pizzas.

GRILLED PORK TENDERLOIN WITH PINEAPPLE SALSA

Pork tenderloin is probably one of the easiest things to prepare on the grill. We were taught for many, many years that pork should be cooked until it is well-done. Today, the rules have changed. A moist and tender 145 to 150°F (63 to 65°C) internal cook temperature has become quite acceptable. Grilling some of the components of the salsa add a smoky touch and brings it all together.

SERVES: 6–8

½ cup (120 ml) pineapple juice

¼ cup (4 g) chopped cilantro

2 cloves garlic, minced

1 tbsp (15 ml) soy sauce

2 scallions, white and light green parts, chopped

2 tbsp (30 ml) olive oil

2 (1-lb [454-g]) pork tenderloins

PINEAPPLE SALSA

½ fresh pineapple, peeled, cored and sliced into rings

½ red onion

1 large red bell pepper

1 jalapeño, diced

½ cup (8 g) chopped cilantro

Juice of ½ lime

¼ tsp ground ginger

¼ tsp ground cumin

Salt and pepper to taste

In a large baking dish, combine the juice, cilantro, garlic, soy sauce, scallions and oil and stir to blend well. Add the tenderloins to the dish and turn to coat in the marinade. Let them marinate for at least 4 hours in the refrigerator.

Preheat the grill to 300°F (150°C).

Remove the tenderloins from the marinade and grill for about 4 minutes per side. Turn them often so they do not char too much, which will make the tenderloins bitter. Check for an internal temperature of 145 to 150°F (63 to 65°C). Pull the pork from the heat and let it rest for 10 minutes before slicing.

To make the salsa, place the pineapple and onion on the grill for a couple of minutes per side to get good grill marks. Cut the pineapple into bite-size chunks and dice the onion. Mix all of the ingredients in a bowl and let the flavors mingle. Slice the tenderloin and serve with the salsa.

BONELESS PORK LOIN CHOP WITH APPLE AND BACON CHUTNEY

Who doesn't love a good pork chop? And what goes with them? Apples! When I was growing up it was applesauce. The secret? Bacon makes everything better. Adding it to the chutney just might send you into a food coma. Be prepared because the apple bacon chutney just may become an addiction.

SERVES: 4

A.1. Bold Original Dry Rub

4 boneless pork chops, cut 1" (2.5 cm) thick

APPLE BACON CHUTNEY

4 slices thick-cut bacon, chopped

4 Gala apples, peeled, cored and diced

½ cup (80 g) diced sweet onion

1 tbsp (6 g) minced fresh ginger

½ cup (120 ml) blood orange juice

¼ cup (60 ml) apple cider vinegar

½ tsp salt

½ tsp apple pie spice

⅓ cup (75 g) packed brown sugar

½ cup (75 g) raisins

Sprinkle the dry rub on both sides of the chops and let them rest in the fridge while you prepare the apple and bacon chutney.

To make the chutney, fry the bacon in a heavy saucepan over medium heat. When the bacon is halfway cooked, drain the grease and add all of the remaining ingredients to the pan. Simmer the chutney, covered, over medium-low heat for 45 minutes or until the majority of the liquid has disappeared, stirring often. Lower the heat and keep it warm until the chops are done.

Preheat the grill to 300°F (150°C).

Grill the chops for 5 minutes on each side, or until they reach 150°F (65°C) on a meat thermometer. Remove the pork chops from the grill and let them rest for 5 minutes to allow the juices inside to set. Slice the chops and serve with the apple bacon chutney spooned over the top.

PORK BELLY BREAKFAST HASH

Breakfast is probably my favorite meal of the day. What's not to love about bacon, eggs, hash browns, flaky biscuits and gravy? Okay, now I'm drooling. I love hash. It's perfect. Meat, potatoes and veggies all in one. The thing that makes this hash special is definitely creating your own smoked pork belly. When I cooked mine I actually used the belly of one of my own hogs. I can get extremely grumpy in the morning if I don't get an egg and "breakfast food." So, let's pour a hot cup of coffee and get this day started right.

SERVES: 4

---

1 cup (200 g) Sugar In The Raw

½ tsp onion powder

1 tsp (2 g) Old Bay Seasoning

2 tbsp (12 g) smoked paprika

1 tsp (2 g) poultry seasoning

½ tsp ground black pepper, plus more to taste

½ tsp salt, plus more to taste

½ tsp chili powder

1 (4-lb [1.8-kg]) uncured pork belly

2 tbsp (30 ml) vegetable oil

3 large russet potatoes, peeled and diced

½ cup (80 g) diced yellow onion

½ cup (75 g) diced bell pepper

1 tsp (3 g) chopped garlic

4 large eggs

½ cup (60 g) shredded Kraft Triple Cheddar Cheese

Combine the sugar, onion powder, Old Bay, paprika, poultry seasoning, ground black pepper, salt and chili powder in a bowl and blend thoroughly. Coat the pork belly with the rub and let it rest at room temperature for 30 minutes.

Preheat the smoker to 250°F (120°C).

Place the belly in the smoker and cook for 3 to 4 hours, depending on the thickness, or until the temperature in the center reaches 160°F (71°C) on a meat thermometer. Pull the belly out of the smoker and let it cool for 30 minutes.

While the belly is cooling, combine the oil and potatoes in a large, heavy skillet. Cover the pan and fry the potatoes over medium heat for 10 minutes, stirring halfway though. Slice the pork belly into ½-inch (1.3-cm) cubes and stir 1½ cups (330 g) into the fried potatoes. If you crave more pork, go for it. Add as much as you like. Stir in the onion, bell pepper and garlic. Cover the pan and fry for another 10 minutes, or until the potatoes are tender. Lower the heat and crack the eggs on top of the hash. Lightly season the eggs with salt and pepper, cover the pan and cook for 5 minutes longer, or until the whites of the eggs are set. Remove from the heat and sprinkle on the shredded cheese.

SLOW-SMOKED BABY BACK PORK RIBS

Pork rib recipes can be a touchy subject to the barbecue enthusiast. Just like belly buttons, everybody has one. To the home cook, the perfect rib is falling off of the bone. Forgive me for I am about to use a four-letter word. Some people "boil" their ribs before they finish them off with the grill and a slather of sauce. There are arguments on dry ribs and wet ribs, sauces, wrapping, techniques, you name it. I'm not publishing my competition ribs—honestly, I don't like competition ribs. They are way too rich for my taste. And if I did, where would that leave me? This recipe is a simple one. It's good for the backyard weekend barbecue god or tailgater who wants to step up their game a bit. My secret? My rubs contain Old Bay. There are those who think I'm a bit strange for that. Also, I add the special wrapping technique. The average Joe doesn't add this step at home or even know about it, but it is something used often by barbecue professionals.

SERVES: 4

---

1 cup (200 g) Sugar In The Raw

½ cup (112 g) packed light brown sugar

1 tbsp (6 g) Old Bay Seasoning

2 tbsp (12 g) smoked paprika

½ tsp onion powder

½ tsp ancho chile powder

½ tsp chipotle powder

2 (2-lb [908-g]) racks baby back pork ribs

Olive oil

Cooking butter spray

Honey

Softened butter in a squeeze bottle

Preheat the smoker to 250°F (120°C).

In a bowl, combine the Sugar In The Raw, light brown sugar, Old Bay, paprika, onion powder, ancho chile powder and chipotle powder. Take a paper towel and remove the membrane from the back of the ribs. This is not edible and it becomes tough. Removing it also helps get the rub into more contact with the meat and penetrate better. Rub the ribs with a light coating of olive oil and apply the rub generously to both sides of the ribs.

Lay the ribs in the smoker and cook for 2 hours, spraying with butter every 30 to 45 minutes to help keep them moist. After 2 hours of smoking, make a wrap for the ribs. Tear off two pieces of foil long enough to wrap each rib. On the foil, sprinkle some of the leftover rub, a line of honey, and a line of softened butter. Lay the ribs in the foil, bottom side up, and wrap them tightly. Place the ribs back in the smoker for another 1½ hours. Open the foil to check for tenderness. Now, I'm not going to tell you what the correct tenderness is. That's up to you. If you want them to where the bone will fall out when you pick them up, then cook them until they reach that point. Cooking time on ribs varies greatly anyway, depending on the thickness of the rib and the amount of fat in it. I'm giving you a guiding hand, but everyone has his or her preference.

HOMEMADE COUNTRY PORK SAUSAGE

I find my mind wandering to the subject of breakfast once again. I know it is extremely easy to walk into your local grocery store and grab your favorite brand of pork breakfast sausage and head home. But making your own is easy and you get to control the ingredients that go into it. What makes this sausage special is the use of fresh herbs. Sausage purchased from the store contains dry seasonings as well as items that we can't even pronounce. I love to raise my own hogs, butcher them myself and make my own sausage. There is nothing sexier than the smell of sausage frying in the kitchen. Well, maybe I can think of one more thing . . . bacon.

SERVES: 10–12

2 lb (908 g) ground pork

1 tsp (1 g) red pepper flakes

5 fresh sage leaves, finely chopped

½ tsp chopped fresh thyme

½ tsp chopped fresh oregano

½ tsp ground black pepper

1 tsp (6 g) kosher salt

2 scallions, white and light green parts, chopped

2 tsp (6 g) chopped garlic

In a large bowl, combine all the ingredients and mix by hand until well blended. Cover the sausage and let it set in the fridge overnight.

The next morning, preheat your grill to 325°F (170°C).

Form the sausage into patties. Grill them until the juices run clear and the middle is no longer pink, 3 to 4 minutes per side. Time will depend on the thickness and size of the patties you make.

GOCHUJANG-BRAISED AND GRILLED BEER BRATS

What person doesn't enjoy a good beer brat? Just like any great dish, the better quality the ingredients, the better the final outcome. Making your own brats may take some practice, but once you get the hang of it you will never again buy a brat at the store. What makes this extra special? The secret beer bath. The addition of the *gochujang*, a spicy Korean condiment, and paprika give the sausages a beautiful color and a distinct heat.

SERVES: 6

SAUSAGE

2 lb (908 g) ground pork

1 lb (454 g) ground veal

1 tbsp (18 g) kosher salt

2 tsp (4 g) white pepper

1 tsp (1 g) dried marjoram

½ tsp caraway seeds

¼ tsp ground ginger

1 tbsp (10 g) chopped garlic

1 shallot, chopped

1 (8-oz [227-g]) package natural sausage casings

BEER BOIL

2 (12-oz [355-ml]) bottles Kentucky Bourbon Barrel Ale

1 tsp (2 g) sweet paprika

1 tbsp (15 g) gochujang

To make the sausage, combine the pork, veal, salt, pepper, marjoram, caraway, ginger, garlic and shallot in a large bowl and mix together by hand. Let it set overnight in the refrigerator. The next morning, prepare the casings as stated on the package directions. Tie off the end of the casing and slide the casing all the way onto the stuffing tube. Slowly let the sausage fill the casing, twisting the sausages every 5 to 6 inches (12.5 to 15.2 cm). When you reach the end of the casing, tie the end off. If the casing breaks during filling, just tie it off and start again.

To make the beer boil, combine the ale, paprika and gochujang in a large saucepan and bring to a simmer. Drop 6 sausages at a time into the boil and simmer over low heat for 10 minutes.

Preheat your grill to 300°F (150°C).

Remove the sausages from the boil and place on the grill for 3 to 4 minutes per side.

TENNESSEE TENDERLOIN (SMOKED BOLOGNA)

Over the years I have played with all sorts of meats, veggies and sweets on the grill and smoker. The first time I heard of smoking a roll of bologna I laughed and thought to myself, *That is about as redneck as it gets.* Of course, that meant I had to give it a try. WOW! That was my first reaction when I saw it finished on the smoker and when I tasted it. I have added this to my menu a few times when I'm out vending. I have to explain to them that it's not pork loin and then I get the "look." The surprise here is the fact that it's bologna, for one thing. But the other is the technique of scoring and dry rubbing it to create the best-tasting bologna you will ever put in your mouth! Don't forget to serve alongside some crackers and mustard. Pass me a beer, please . . .

SERVES: 10–15

1 (5-lb [2.3-kg]) roll bologna (or any size roll or brand you like)

2–3 tbsp (22–33 g) Dijon mustard

RUB
1 cup (225 g) packed light brown sugar

½ tsp onion powder

1 tsp (2 g) Old Bay Seasoning

2 tbsp (12 g) smoked paprika

½ tsp chipotle powder

½ tsp ground black pepper

½ tsp kosher salt

½ tsp chili powder

½ tsp garlic powder

Prepare your grill for two-zone cooking. If you are using a charcoal grill, burn the charcoal on only one side of your grill. Fire up your grill to 250°F (120°C). I love to add cherry and hickory woods when I'm smoking the bologna for extra color and flavor.

Score the roll of bologna with a sharp paring knife. This helps get more rub and smoke penetration. Rub the outside with the mustard to cover the entire surface. This adds flavor and provides a good base for the rub to adhere to.

To make the rub, combine all the ingredients in a small bowl. Spread the rub mixture over the entire surface of the bologna. I like a thick covering to get a crisp outside.

Smoke the bologna over indirect heat for 3 hours. The outside will be a beautiful mahogany and crisp. This is delicious sliced for sandwiches or eaten on crackers.

GRILLED PINEAPPLE PULLED PORK SANDWICHES

Most every barbecue fanatic will proclaim his or her pork is the best there is. I mean, come on—we take great pride in what we do. I have been told that this recipe is "just wrong" because it isn't a traditional pulled pork sandwich. But, if you are feeling adventurous one weekend, let go of what you know and give it a whirl. The secret is the addition of the grilled pineapple paired with the creamy slaw. It adds sweetness and another level of texture. I like to feed folks very well. My sandwiches are loaded with about ½ pound (227 g) of yummy pork.

SERVES: 10–12

---

1 (8- to 10-lb [3.6- to 4.5-kg]) pork butt

RUB

Apple juice, for injecting

1 cup (225 g) packed light brown sugar

½ cup (100 g) sugar in the raw

1 tbsp (6 g) Old Bay Seasoning

⅓ cup (32 g) smoked paprika

½ tsp chili powder

½ tsp onion powder

½ tsp salt

SLAW

1 (1-lb [454-g]) package slaw mix

⅓ cup (80 g) mayonnaise

⅛ tsp celery salt

2 tbsp (25 g) granulated sugar

2 tbsp (30 ml) apple cider vinegar

10–12 pineapple slices

10–12 brioche buns

Heat your smoker to 250°F (120°C). I love to use cherry and hickory woods when I smoke my pork, but you can play with different woods, such as oak, for different flavor profiles.

Inject your pork butt with as much apple juice as you can pump into it. Let it rest for half an hour.

Meanwhile, to make the rub, combine the brown sugar, sugar in the raw, Old Bay, paprika, chili powder, onion powder and salt in a small bowl. Coat the pork butt with a layer of the rub.

Smoke the butt for 4 hours and then wrap it in foil. After 4 more hours do a temperature check. The total cooking time will depend on the weight of your pork butt and the quality. Most butts are ready to pull once a thermometer inserted into the center reads 195°F (91°C). The pork will need to rest for at least an hour to cool down enough to pull.

To make the slaw, combine the slaw mix, mayonnaise, celery salt, granulated sugar and vinegar in a large bowl. Toss to mix well.

Right before serving, grill off your pineapple slices over medium heat for 2 minutes on each side. Pull the pork butt and mix in 2 tablespoons (12 g) of the remaining rub. Build your sandwich by placing the pork, a slice of grilled pineapple and some slaw on the bun.

COUNTRY HAM HONEY MUSTARD SLIDERS

It's true that I like to be in control all of the time. My viewing party for episodes of *American Grilled* was no different. I designed the menu, cooked the food and set up the buffet. These country ham sliders were a huge hit. I know you may say it's just a ham sandwich. The secret to what makes this one special is the technique. By placing the assembled slider back on the grill, it crisps up the outside and gives it a meringue-like texture and sweetness. They may be extremely simple, but sometimes the simple things bring the most pleasure.

SERVES: 12

1 lb (454 g) Blue Grass country ham, thinly sliced

1 (12-oz [340-g]) package King's Hawaiian Sweet Rolls

1 lb (454 g) baby Swiss cheese, thinly sliced

O'Charley's Honey Mustard

Honey

Prepare your grill for two-zone cooking. If you are using a charcoal grill, burn the charcoal on only one side of your grill. If you have a gas grill, only light one side of your burners. Preheat the grill to 275°F (135°C).

Quickly grill the country ham to crisp it up. Split the rolls and place some ham, cheese and honey mustard on each. Place the top on each roll and place them in a baking dish. Cook over indirect heat for 5 minutes. Drizzle honey over the sandwiches after they come off the grill. Lawd, have mercy! These little nuggets of salty sweetness will disappear as fast as you get them off the grill. Make a double batch to be safe.

SMOKED GREEK GYRO

There are some foods that we love to eat when we dine out. For me, the gyro is one of those treats, mainly because it's not something I thought was easy to make at home. Well, I became a girl on a mission. I researched and hunted until I found a recipe that I could duplicate at home and give me a fix for my craving. The secret to this recipe is to make sure the meats are worked to a mush. Once formed and cooked, the mixture becomes the correct solid texture for slicing.

SERVES: 6

1¼ lb (568 g) ground lamb

1¼ lb (568 g) ground beef

3 cloves garlic, minced

2½ tsp (5 g) onion powder

4 tsp (4 g) dried oregano

1 tsp (2 g) ground black pepper

2 tsp (12 g) salt

¾ cup (75 g) plain bread crumbs

6 pita breads

Sliced red onion

Chopped romaine lettuce

Greek Yogurt Sauce (page 84)

Preheat your smoker to 300°F (150°C).

In the bowl of a food processor, combine the lamb, beef, garlic, onion powder, oregano, pepper, salt and bread crumbs and process until the mixture is smooth. If you don't have a food processor you can do the same by kneading the mixture with your hands as if you were kneading bread dough. Form the mixture into a square loaf 3 inches (7.6 cm) thick.

Smoke the loaf for an hour and 15 minutes. Remove the loaf and allow it to cool for 10 minutes before slicing thin. Serve the slices in the pita bread with the red onion and romaine lettuce and drizzle with the yogurt sauce.

GRILLED LAMB BURGERS

Just because I'm from Kentucky doesn't mean I'm a fan of mutton. Quite honestly, it makes me gag. But when it comes to lamb, well, that's another story. This is one juicy, flavor-packed burger. The secret is the addition of the ground pork. It lends moisture to the burger from the fat and mellows the lamb. I do nothing ordinary, so if you don't think you like lamb I assure you that you must give this a try.

SERVES: 4

GREEK YOGURT SAUCE

1 cup (225 g) plain yogurt

1 cup (225 g) sour cream

1 tsp (5 ml) lemon juice

1 small cucumber, peeled and finely chopped

¼ cup (40 g) diced red onion

2 cloves garlic, minced

⅓ cup (50 g) crumbled feta cheese

¼ tsp oregano

Salt and pepper to taste

BURGERS

1 lb (454 g) ground lamb

½ lb (227 g) ground pork

2 tbsp (12 g) chopped scallion

2 tsp (4 g) Greek seasoning

4 brioche buns

4 slices tomato

Sliced red onion

Arugula

To make the sauce, combine all the ingredients in a medium-size bowl, cover and refrigerate overnight.

To make the burgers, combine the lamb, pork, scallion and Greek seasoning in a large bowl. Form the mixture into 4 patties and let them rest while you heat up the grill.

Preheat the grill to 275°F (135°C).

Cook the burgers for 5 minutes on each side, until the juices run clear or the internal temperature reaches 155°F (68°C) on a meat thermometer. Let the burgers rest for 5 minutes.

Place a burger on the bottom of each bun and top with a slice of tomato, onion and arugula. Drizzle with the yogurt sauce. Make sure you have a napkin ready.

RACK OF LAMB WITH ROASTED BEET AND TOMATO SALAD

For some, this dish may seem like an odd combination, but the flavors complement each other very well. The secret to this dish is the slight gamey flavor of the lamb combined with the sweet earthiness of the beets, the acidity of the tomatoes and the saltiness of the feta and olives.

SERVES: 4–6

---

1 (1½–2 lb [680–908 g]) rack of lamb

2 cloves garlic, finely minced

2 tbsp (4 g) chopped fresh rosemary

2 scallions, white and green parts, chopped

2 tbsp (4 g) chopped fresh thyme

1 tbsp (11 g) Dijon mustard

2 tbsp (30 ml) white wine

4 beets, blanched, peeled and diced

¼ cup (40 g) diced red onion

2 tbsp (30 ml) balsamic vinegar

1 cup (150 g) mixed mini tomatoes, halved

¼ cup (25 g) kalamata olives

½ cup (75 g) crumbled feta cheese

Place the lamb in a large zip-top bag. In a bowl, combine the garlic, rosemary, scallion, thyme, mustard and white wine. Stir to blend well, and then pour over the lamb. Seal the bag, toss the lamb around in the marinade and let it chill in the refrigerator for 4 hours.

Prepare your grill for two-zone cooking. If you are using a charcoal grill, burn the charcoal on only one side of your grill. If you have a gas grill, only light one side of your burners. Preheat your grill to 275°F (135°C).

Place the beets in a baking dish. Roast them over indirect heat until they are tender, 10 to 15 minutes. Toss in the red onion, balsamic vinegar, tomatoes and olives. Let the mixture roast for 5 minutes longer. Remove the beet mixture from the grill and allow it to cool.

Grill the lamb over the same grill but using direct heat for about 8 minutes per side, or until the internal temperature reaches 145°F (63°C) on a meat thermometer. The outside will be beautifully marked while the inside will be a perfect pink. Remove the lamb from the heat and allow it to rest for 5 minutes before slicing it.

When it's time to serve, toss the feta cheese in with the beet salad and serve alongside the lamb.

CUBAN-INSPIRED PULLED LEG OF LAMB

If you hadn't figured it out yet, I'm a fan of big flavor. The sauce for the lamb will have your taste buds thinking you are on vacation in a foreign land. I never get tired of my pulled pork, but sometimes it's good to step back from the usual. The secret, as they say, is all in the sauce. Because it cooks in the same pan as the lamb, it imparts more flavor to the lamb itself. Serve the lamb over rice with a good crusty bread.

SERVES: 6

---

1 (4- to 5-lb [1816- to 2270-g]) boneless leg of lamb

Weber Thai Chili Seasoning

2 (8-oz [227-g]) cans tomato sauce

1 green bell pepper, cored, seeded and diced

6 cloves garlic, minced

Juice from 1 lime

1 sweet onion, diced

1 (4-oz [113-g]) can diced green chilies

2 tbsp (32 g) tomato paste

2 tbsp (6 g) dried Mexican oregano

1 tbsp (6 g) ground cumin

⅓ cup (5 g) fresh cilantro, chopped

Salt and pepper to taste

Preheat your smoker to 250°F (120°C).

Rub the outside of the lamb with the Thai chili seasoning. Place the lamb in the smoker and let it soak up smoke for 2 hours. Remove the lamb from the smoker and place it in a deep roasting pan. Combine the remaining ingredients and pour them over the leg of lamb. Cover the pan with foil and place it back in the smoker. After 4 hours, check the lamb for doneness by using two forks to see if it will pull apart and shred easily. The whole cooking time could take up to 6 hours, depending on the size of the leg of lamb. Once the lamb is easily shredded, combine it well with the sauce in the pan.

ROCK STAR SEAFOOD DISHES

"COOKING IS LIKE LOVE. IT SHOULD BE ENTERED INTO WITH ABANDON OR NOT AT ALL."

—HARRIET VAN HORNE

Seafood can be a scary thing to prepare. We sometimes fear we will over- or undercook it. Nevertheless, I still love to make it as much as I love to eat it. Seafood is a terrific landscape for fresh ingredients and bold flavors. When we are children, we think seafood refers to fish sticks or popcorn shrimp. But as adults, we learn that it means so much more. There is a whole symphony of seafood out there for us to masterfully orchestrate.

FIRECRACKER SHRIMP TACOS WITH AVOCADO SALSA

I love shrimp and I love tacos. The thought of bringing these two different things together makes the clouds part and the angels sing its praises. Fresh raw shrimp is a must. Frozen shrimp contain too much water and will not cook properly. Be careful: Shrimp cook very fast and will become tough. The secret to grilling shrimp is to put them on skewers so turning them will be a breeze. The cabbage brings a texture to the dish that is essential.

SERVES: 4

AVOCADO SALSA

2 ripe avocados, peeled, pitted and diced

¼ cup (40 g) diced red onion

1 jalapeño, seeded and diced

2 tbsp (2 g) chopped cilantro

2 tbsp (30 ml) lime juice

2 cloves garlic, minced

Salt and pepper to taste

SHRIMP TACOS

1 lb (454 g) medium-large (38 ct) raw shrimp, cleaned

¼ cup (60 ml) olive oil

1 tbsp (10 g) chopped garlic

1 cup (16 g) chopped cilantro

Juice from 1 lime

1 tbsp (15 ml) white wine

¾ cup (180 ml) Frank's RedHot Sweet Chili Sauce

16 soft shell tacos

1 cup (90 g) chopped napa cabbage

To make the salsa, combine all of the ingredients in a medium-size bowl, toss to blend and store in a tightly sealed container in the refrigerator until it's time to assemble the tacos.

To make the shrimp tacos, in a large zip-top bag, combine the shrimp, olive oil, garlic, cilantro, lime juice and white wine. Let the shrimp marinate for an hour in the fridge and then thread them onto skewers.

Preheat the grill to 300°F (150°C).

Grill the skewers for around 3 minutes on each side, or until pink. Pull the shrimp off the skewers, place in a bowl and lightly toss with the sweet chili sauce. Place the shrimp in the taco shells and serve topped with the avocado salsa and napa cabbage.

LOBSTER MASHED POTATOES

The big trend in restaurants right now is lobster mac and cheese. I'm not one to do as others do. I am a meat and taters kinda girl, so naturally that's the direction I went. The secret to great roasted garlic is to cut the top off of a whole garlic bulb, place it in foil, drizzle it with olive oil, sprinkle it with salt and pepper and roast it until it becomes soft and caramelized. If you want to play the surf and turf card, why not pair this dish with a steak? Now you're talking my language.

SERVES: 4

2 (6-oz [168-g]) lobster tails

⅓ cup (80 ml) unsalted butter, melted

½ tsp Zatarain's Creole Seasoning

ROASTED GARLIC MASHED POTATOES

1½ lb (680 g) Yukon gold potatoes

½ tsp salt

2 tbsp (29 g) Land O' Lakes unsalted sweet cream butter

¼ cup (60 ml) heavy cream or as needed

1 tsp (1 g) chopped chives, plus 1 tsp (1 g) for garnish

3 cloves roasted garlic (see Note, page 18)

4 slices bacon, chopped

½ cup (60 g) shredded Kraft Triple Cheddar Cheese

Preheat your grill to 275°F (140°C).

Using a sharp knife, slice the lobster tails down through the middle but make sure not to cut all the way through. Open the lobster as if you were opening a book. Spread butter on the flesh, sprinkle on the seasoning and grill the tail, flesh side up, for 5 minutes. Baste the meat with more butter and continue grilling for another 5 minutes, or until the internal temperature at the thickest part reaches 135°F (57°C) on a meat thermometer. Remove the lobster from the heat and let cool.

To make the mashed potatoes, peel and quarter the potatoes. Place them in a heavy saucepan and cover them with water. Cover the pan and bring the potatoes to a simmer over medium heat. Let the potatoes cook for 15 to 20 minutes, or until a fork goes through them easily. Drain the potatoes and add the rest of the mashed potato ingredients. Blend on medium speed with a handheld blender until they are light and fluffy.

Remove the lobster from the shells and chop the lobster meat. Carefully fold the lobster into the potatoes. What will make these even better? Garnishing with some chopped bacon, chopped chives and shredded cheese, of course.

SPINACH AND ARTICHOKE GRILLED OYSTERS

I love raw oysters with a little hot sauce or cocktail sauce, fried oysters and most certainly grilled oysters. The secret to a fantastic oyster is to pick ones that are large and tightly closed. If it is open, stay away from it. I have had oysters grilled with Parmesan and crispy spinach. But, I got to thinking, why not with warm and gooey spinach and artichoke dip? Fresh oysters . . . warm and melty cheese . . . YES, PLEASE. Yes, my brain is always working like that.

SERVES: 4

SPINACH AND ARTICHOKE DIP

½ cup (50 g) freshly shredded Parmesan cheese

¾ cup (90 g) grated pepper Jack cheese

¾ cup (90 g) grated Gruyère cheese

1 (10-oz [280-g]) package frozen chopped spinach

1 (14-oz [392-g]) jar or can artichoke hearts, chopped

1 (8-oz [227-g]) package cream cheese, cubed

⅔ cup (160 g) sour cream

⅓ cup (80 g) Duke's mayonnaise

2 tsp (6 g) chopped garlic

12 raw oysters on the half shell

½ cup (60 g) panko bread crumbs, for topping

Preheat your smoker to 275°F (140°C). Preheat the grill to 300°F (150°C).

To make the dip, combine all of the ingredients in a baking dish and smoke, uncovered, for 22 to 30 minutes, or until the cheeses are melted and bubbly. Allow it to set and cool for 10 minutes.

Top the raw oysters with the dip and sprinkle each one with some of the panko. Grill the oysters until the juices begin to bubble, about 5 minutes. Serve the oysters warm and right away.

GINGER PECAN BOURBON GLAZED SALMON

I like to cook with alcohol . . . and use it in my dishes, too. Salmon is a very good palette to work with. I like to prepare my salmon with just a touch of sweetness. Some folks go Asian, but I think brown sugar and bourbon. The trick is to pack the nut mixture firmly onto the salmon, and it will become a candy-like topping. I have been told that this is the best salmon recipe that some have ever tasted. I'll let you judge that one for yourself.

SERVES: 4

4 (4-oz [112-g]) portions salmon fillet

McCormick's Grill Mates Brown Sugar and Bourbon Seasoning

Sweet Bourbon Glaze (page 17)

1 cup (145 g) chopped pecans

½ tsp grated ginger

Generously coat the salmon with the brown sugar and bourbon seasoning. Place in a dish and allow the salmon to marinate in the fridge for 1 hour.

Prepare your grill for two-zone cooking. If you are using a charcoal grill, burn the charcoal on only one side of your grill. If you have a gas grill, only light one side of your burners. Preheat your grill to 275°F (140°C) using lump charcoal and cherry wood chunks.

Combine the bourbon glaze, pecans and ginger in a small bowl and pack the mixture on top of the salmon fillets. Place the salmon on the grill over indirect heat and cook until the fat starts to render from the fish, 5 to 8 minutes. I know it's not very healthy, but just keep telling yourself that you're eating salmon and it's all good.

GRILLED RAINBOW TROUT WITH GOETTA STUFFING

This is another recipe that was born from my appearance on *American Grilled*. Most people panic when they have a whole fish given to them. If you aren't used to breaking down fish, it can be quite intimidating. That didn't bother me. My biggest decision was whether to fillet it or to leave it whole. Well, I guess I made the right decision because I lived to see the next round. The secret ingredient has to be the goetta, a lightly seasoned pork sausage made with steel-cut oats. Trout doesn't take very long to cook and it is an extremely delicate fish. If you are afraid it may fall apart on you, then try grilling it in a fish basket.

SERVES: 2

1 recipe Sweet Bourbon Glaze (page 17)

¼ tsp soy sauce

2 (3- to 4-oz [84- to 112-g]) rainbow trout fillets

Olive oil

Salt and pepper to taste

GOETTA STUFFING

1 (1-lb [454-g]) package Glier's goetta

½ cup (35 g) sliced button mushrooms

½ cup (80 g) diced sweet onion

2 tbsp (30 ml) olive oil

1 tsp (2 g) poultry seasoning

½ tsp chipotle powder

6 cornbread muffins

Chicken stock or water, as needed

Preheat your grill to 300°F (150°C).

In a bowl, combine the bourbon glaze with the soy sauce and set aside. Coat the trout on all sides with olive oil to keep it from sticking to the grill grates. Lightly season the fish with salt and pepper. Grill the fish, skin side down, for about 6 minutes, or until the fish is flaky and the skin is crisp. After 2 minutes, brush the fish with the glaze.

To make the stuffing, combine the goetta, mushrooms, onion, olive oil, poultry seasoning and chipotle powder in a saucepan over medium heat. Stir the mixture constantly until the onions and mushrooms are tender, 5 to 10 minutes. Crumble in the cornbread muffins and stir. If the stuffing is a little dry you can add a little stock to moisten it. Remove the stuffing from the heat.

Serve the trout on a bed of the stuffing. Don't be like me and get a little heavy-handed with the chipotle, or you may need some extra sweet tea handy.

GARLIC AND HERB-GRILLED SNOW CRAB FRIES WITH KENTUCKY ALE WHITE BEER CHEESE

I have eaten a lot of crab legs and I have found that my favorite is snow crab. Many places boil or steam their crabs and you are stuck paying for overpriced crab with no flavor whatsoever. How can you top grilling your own crab? By placing it as a glorious crown atop crispy French fries smothered in Kentucky beer cheese! Don't faint now, y'all. Stay home and cook you some snow crab that you will actually enjoy—and you won't need a reservation.

SERVES: 4

½ cup (120 ml) olive oil

½ cup (112 g) unsalted butter, melted

2 tbsp (12 g) Old Bay with Garlic & Herb Seasoning plus 1 tsp (2 g) to season fries

2 lb (908 g) snow crab legs

1 (2-lb [908-g]) package natural-cut fries

1 recipe Kentucky Ale White Beer Cheese (page 55), kept warm

8 slices peppered bacon, cooked and chopped

2 scallions, chopped

Preheat your grill to 350°F (180°C).

Combine the oil, melted butter and seasoning in a small bowl. Grill the crab legs and baste with the mixture. Turn a few times, basting on every turn. Cook until the shells start to brown, about 5 minutes. Remove the crab legs and allow them to cool enough to handle. Crack the shells, remove the meat and chop.

Prepare the fries according to package directions and season them with the Old Bay. Top the fries with the beer cheese and crabmeat and garnish with the peppered bacon and scallions. You might need a bib from the drool running down the side of your mouth.

GRILLED TUNA BURGERS WITH ROASTED RED PEPPER MAYO

Growing up, the only tuna I ate was from a can and in the form of tuna salad. As an adult, I fell in love with fresh tuna and seafood. I'm a huge burger fan. Who doesn't appreciate grabbing ahold with both hands and sinking their teeth in? But combining the two? Crazy, maybe. This tuna burger is great if you want to eat a little healthier. Make sure to use fresh tuna and that you pulse it enough so that the fish will hold together when you make the patties. The secret's in the red pepper mayo!

SERVES: 4

TUNA BURGERS

2 lb (908 g) fresh tuna

2 tbsp (30 ml) olive oil

¼ tsp black pepper

½ tsp kosher salt

3 cloves garlic, minced

1 tbsp (15 ml) lemon juice

1 tbsp (10 g) diced pimento

ROASTED RED PEPPER MAYONNAISE

1 (12-oz [340-g]) jar roasted red peppers or 2 freshly roasted red peppers

2 tsp (6 g) chopped garlic

½ cup (115 g) Duke's mayonnaise

3 tbsp (45 ml) extra virgin olive oil

Kosher salt and pepper to taste

4 brioche buns

Arugula

Thinly sliced red onion

Preheat your grill to 300°F (150°C) and oil the grates.

To make the burgers, cube the fresh tuna and add it to a food processor along with the olive oil, pepper, salt, garlic, lemon juice and pimento. Pulse the mixture a few times until it is finely minced. Form the tuna mixture into 4 patties. Place the patties on the grill and cook for 3 to 4 minutes on each side.

To make the mayonnaise, remove the peppers from the jar and pat dry with a paper towel. Chop the peppers and add them to a food processor along with the garlic and mayonnaise. Blend the mixture briefly, and then, with the processor running, drizzle in the olive oil. If the mixture is too thin, add more mayonnaise. Season with salt and pepper to taste.

To assemble, grill the buns, add a tuna patty and top with the arugula, red onion and a dollop of the red pepper mayonnaise.

ASIAN GRILLED TUNA STEAK WITH UDON NOODLES

Udon noodles seem to be my go-to dish lately. I find myself preparing them at least twice a week. I love spice, and these noodles are no exception. Don't worry—they won't set you on fire. The Asian flavors of the tuna marinade and the noodles are perfect together. The secret ingredients that make this special are the sambal and the gochujang. These two flavors paired with cilantro will blow your mind.

SERVES: 2

MARINADE

1 clove garlic, grated

1 tbsp (15 ml) lime juice

¼ cup (60 ml) soy sauce

2 tbsp (30 ml) sesame oil

2 (3- to 4-oz [84- to 112-g]) tuna steaks

UDON NOODLES

1 (1-lb [454-g]) package fresh udon noodles

1 cup (235 ml) chicken stock

¼ cup (4 g) chopped cilantro

1 tsp (3 g) sambal

1 tsp (3 g) gochujang

1 tbsp (6 g) Weber Thai Chili Seasoning

Juice from ½ lime

1 mini bok choy, chopped

1 scallion, white and light green parts, chopped, for garnish

1 tbsp (8 g) sesame seeds, for garnish

Preheat the grill to 300°F (150°C) and oil the grates.

To make the marinade, combine the ingredients in a shallow bowl. Place the tuna in the bowl with the marinade and let sit for 15 minutes, then turn to marinate the other side. Grill the tuna steaks for 3 minutes on each side. Remove them from the heat and let them rest until you have the noodles prepared.

To make the noodles, combine the ingredients in a saucepan over medium heat and bring it to a simmer. Cook the noodles for 5 minutes. Remove the pan from the heat and let the noodles rest for 10 minutes.

Divide the noodles between 2 bowls. Slice the tuna steaks and place one steak in each bowl. Garnish with the chopped scallion and sesame seeds.

SWEET THAI CHILI MAHI MAHI WITH ASIAN SLAW

The citric flavors of lime give the mahi mahi a great flavor. The crisp slaw brightens this dish and helps cleanse the palate. This will soon be your new go-to fish recipe.

SERVES: 2

ASIAN SLAW

2 cloves garlic, minced

2 tbsp (30 ml) soy sauce

2 tbsp (30 ml) rice vinegar

2 tbsp (25 g) sugar

1 tsp (3 g) sambal

1 (1-lb [454-g]) bag slaw mix

3 scallions, white and light green parts, chopped

2 (4-oz [112-g]) mahi mahi fillets

2 tbsp (20 g) Weber Thai Chili Seasoning

Juice of 1 lime

⅓ cup (30 g) chopped cilantro

1 tsp (3 g) sesame seeds, for garnish

To make the slaw, combine the garlic, soy sauce, rice vinegar, sugar and sambal in a large bowl. Add the slaw mix and scallions and toss to coat with the dressing. Cover the slaw and let it marinate in the refrigerator for at least 2 hours.

Rub the fish with the Thai Chili Seasoning. Place the fish into a ziplock bag and add the lime juice and the cilantro. Let the fillets marinate for 30 minutes.

Preheat the grill to 275°F (135°C) and oil the grates.

Grill the fish on each side for 5 minutes, or until the fish flakes when tested with a fork. Place a mound of slaw on each of 2 plates and top with a fish fillet. Garnish with the sesame seeds.

GRILLED BEER-STEAMED MUSSELS

Mussels are just plain fun to eat. The meat inside is succulent and sweet, and the shell can be used to slurp up the delicious broth. Every recipe you find for steamed mussels is created using white wine or stock. Using beer is what makes this extra special. Don't forget to serve with a crusty bread to sop up the juices.

SERVES: 2

1 (1-lb [454-g]) bag mussels

4 cloves garlic, minced

1 small bunch Italian parsley, chopped

Juice of 1 lime

¼ cup (40 g) diced sweet onion

3 tbsp (45 ml) olive oil

1 (12-oz [355-ml]) bottle Kentucky Bourbon Barrel Ale

Light a full chimney starter filled with lump charcoal and when the coals are white and ashy add them to your grill.

Wash the mussels and add them along with all the other ingredients to a Dutch oven. Place the Dutch oven directly over the hot coals. As the sauce in the pot heats up, spoon it over the mussels. As the mussels cook they will begin to open. Once they are fully open, remove the pot from the heat, around 5 minutes. Discard any mussels that fail to open.

KICKED-UP COUNTRY SIDES

"THE ONLY REAL STUMBLING BLOCK IS FEAR OF FAILURE. IN COOKING YOU'VE GOT TO HAVE A 'WHAT THE HELL' ATTITUDE."

–JULIA CHILD

Sometimes I think the side dishes are what make the meal. I can eat mac and cheese as a meal by itself. Meat may be the main focus of the presentation at the table, but to me the sides are the stars.

SUPER CHEESY MAC AND CHEESE

Everyone in the world loves mac and cheese. Well, I suppose if you are lactose intolerant, you may not. But, most people's love affair with cheese started as a small child. We all craved the stuff in the blue box. I'm sure it still conjures up great memories for many. The secret here is adding nacho cheese, which lends a slight heat and creaminess. This is for the child in us all—may we never grow up.

SERVES: 6–8

2 cups (210 g) elbow macaroni

2½ cups (590 ml) milk

½ cup (120 ml) nacho cheese

1 cup (120 g) shredded Kraft Triple Cheddar Cheese

1 cup (120 g) shredded Gouda cheese

3 tbsp (42 g) unsalted butter

½ tsp kosher salt

½ tsp ground black pepper

Preheat the smoker to 275°F (135°C) and grease a 9 x 9-inch (23 x 23-cm) baking dish.

Bring a large stockpot of salted water to a boil, add the noodles and cook according to the package directions.

While the noodles cook, warm the milk and cheeses in a saucepan. Whisk over medium-low heat until the cheese is fully melted. Add the butter, salt and pepper to the cheese sauce and turn off the heat. When the pasta is tender, drain the water from the pot and stir in the cheese sauce.

Pour the mac and cheese into the prepared baking dish. Place in the smoker and bake the mac for about 30 minutes, or until golden.

ROASTED TURNIP AND YUKON GOLD MASHED POTATOES

Mashed potatoes are one side dish that goes with just about everything. There are some weeks that I have requests for them three times. It can become boring serving the same mash. I always remembered my grandma serving roasted turnips every now and then. I would go out to the garden, pull one up and take a big bite of it raw. The secrets to this dish are the roasted turnips and the horseradish. They bring a whole new dimension of flavor to the creamy, rich potatoes. This may make you rethink your whole existence.

SERVES: 4–6

2 turnips, peeled and cubed

Olive oil

Kosher salt and freshly ground black pepper

1½ lb (680 g) Yukon gold potatoes, peeled and cubed

1 tsp (1 g) chopped chives

2 cloves roasted garlic (see Note, page 18)

1 tbsp (10 g) creamy horseradish

1 (3.95-oz [111-g]) package Sargento Tastings Aged Vermont White Cheddar Cheese, grated

3 tbsp (42 g) unsalted butter

½ cup (120 ml) milk, or more as needed, warmed but not boiling

⅓ cup (80 ml) heavy cream

Preheat the grill to 300°F (150°C).

Place the turnips in a small oven-safe dish, drizzle with olive oil, season with a pinch of salt and pepper and cover tightly with foil. Roast the turnips over indirect heat for 30 minutes, or until soft.

Add the potatoes to a large pot and cover with water. Season with 1 teaspoon (6 g) of kosher salt. Bring the water to a boil, then reduce the heat and simmer for 20 minutes, or until a fork goes through easily. Drain the potatoes, return them to the pot and add your roasted turnips. Mash by hand with a potato masher until the mix is creamy. Add the chives, roasted garlic, horseradish, white cheddar, butter, milk and heavy cream. Mash until everything is well-blended. If the mash is too thick for you, just add a little warm milk until you get the consistency you want. Season with salt and pepper to taste.

SOUTHERN-STYLE KENTUCKY WONDER GREEN BEANS

I remember as a little girl sitting on a bucket in the garden alongside my grandma, picking beans and then snapping them as we sat on the front porch. It was a labor of love. She would season them with crispy fried bacon and the yummy bacon drippings, and then simmer them for hours on the stovetop. I have found a way to make canned green beans taste as if I toiled away preparing them all day. No one can ever believe these came from a can when they taste them. The secret to making these beans taste home-grown is the chicken stock, seasoning and cooking method. No one has to know how easy these are to make. It can be our little secret.

SERVES: 4–6

---

2 (14.4-oz [403-g]) cans Kentucky Wonder style green beans

4 slices thick-cut bacon

⅓ cup (53 g) diced sweet onion

1 tbsp (6 g) Montreal Steak Seasoning

½ cup (120 ml) chicken stock

Prepare your grill for two-zone cooking. If you are using a charcoal grill, burn the charcoal on only one side of your grill. If you have a gas grill, only light one side of your burners. Preheat the grill to 325°F (170°C) and grease a 9 x 13-inch (23 x 33-cm) baking dish.

Drain the green beans and empty them into the prepared baking dish. Fry the bacon slices in a skillet until crispy, remove from the skillet, reserving 1 teaspoon (5 ml) of the drippings, and drain the bacon on a paper towel–lined plate. Crumble the bacon into the green beans and stir in the reserved drippings. Add the onion, seasoning and stock to the green beans and stir to combine. Place the baking dish, uncovered, on the grill over indirect heat and cook for 1 hour, or until there is some crisp on top. Remove the green beans from the heat and give them a stir. Serve warm.

BBQ VOLCANO POTATOES

One of the new fads on the barbecue scene is the volcano potato. These are basically a new take on a twice-baked potato. Most are stuffed with deli turkey and cheese. Well, you should know by now that I don't follow the norm. These mouthwatering flavor bombs get their name from the topper of cheese that flows down over the sides and the volcano sauce that adds the final touch. The secret is definitely in the filling that hides within the walls of the potato.

SERVES: 4

4 large baking potatoes

TACO SEASONING

1 tbsp (6 g) Mexican chili powder

1 tsp (2 g) ground cumin

1 tsp (2 g) garlic powder

1 tsp (2 g) sweet paprika

½ tsp Mexican oregano

½ tsp onion powder

¼ tsp salt

¼ tsp ground black pepper

¼ tsp red pepper flakes

1 lb (454 g) ground chuck

⅓ cup (60 g) Rotel tomatoes with chiles

8 slices bacon

¾ cup (90 g) Kraft Mexican Blend Shredded Cheese

½ cup (112 g) sour cream

1 tbsp (15 ml) hot taco sauce

2 tbsp (12 g) chopped scallion

Prepare your grill for two-zone cooking. If you are using a charcoal grill, burn the charcoal on only one side of your grill. If you have a gas grill, only light one side of your burners. Preheat the grill to 325°F (170°C).

Wash the potatoes and poke a fork into the center of each potato to allow steam to escape. Wrap each potato in aluminum foil and place them over direct heat. Let the potatoes roast for about 45 minutes. The size of the potato you use will affect the roasting time. The potatoes are done when a knife inserted into the center goes in with no resistance. Allow the potatoes to cool until they are easy to handle.

To make the taco seasoning, combine all the ingredients in a bowl.

Brown the ground chuck in a skillet over medium-high heat until it is no longer pink, around 10 minutes. Drain the grease from the skillet and add 2 tablespoons (12 g) of your taco spice mixture to the ground chuck along with the tomatoes. Let the mixture simmer for 5 minutes.

Next, cut the bottom off of each potato, about ½ inch (1.3 cm), so the potatoes sit flat. With a knife, cut the top off of each potato and carefully scoop out the center of the potato with a small spoon. Some cooks use an apple corer to make this easier. Wrap 2 slices of bacon around each potato, leaving the top open. You may use toothpicks to secure the bacon around the potatoes. Spoon some of the meat filling into each potato.

Make sure your grill is still holding at 325°F (170°C). If not, add more coals. Place the potatoes back on the grill over indirect heat for around 35 minutes. Top the potatoes with the shredded cheese in a tall pile on each. Allow them to cook for another 10 minutes, or until the cheese is melted and flowing over the sides.

Right before serving, mix the sour cream and taco sauce together in a small bowl. Top the potatoes with the sour cream mixture and sprinkle on the scallions. BOOM! Potato explosion on the taste buds.

SWEET AND TANGY APPLE COLESLAW

Where you live will pretty much define what kind of slaw your taste buds prefer. I grew up with a bowl of vinegar slaw on the kitchen table every evening with supper. Even though I have very fond memories of those meals, my slaw of choice is a perfect combination of sweet and creamy with a touch of tartness. The secret is the crunch of the apples and the hint of smoke from the mayo that make this recipe a unique and refreshing side dish. This slaw pairs perfectly with any meat, whether you serve it with fried chicken, barbecue or whatever wild game you harvested while hunting this morning. This recipe is a keeper for sure.

SERVES: 6–8

COLESLAW

3 Gala apples, diced

1 cup (150 g) red seedless grapes, halved

2 lb (908 g) prepared coleslaw mix

⅓ cup (80 ml) apple cider vinegar

⅛ tsp celery salt

1 tsp (3 g) Dijon mustard

1 tsp (1 g) ranch salad dressing powder

SMOKED MAYO

3 egg yolks

1 tbsp (15 ml) lemon juice

¼ tsp salt

¼ tsp dry mustard

Pinch of cayenne pepper

1½ cup (355 ml) light flavor olive oil

2 tbsp (30 ml) hot water

Preheat the smoker to a cool 85°F (29°C). Place the egg yolks in a bowl and place that bowl in another bowl full of ice. Place the bowls in the smoker and cold smoke for 5 minutes. The yolks should still be cold and not cooked. Place the yolks in a food processor on low and add the remaining ingredients in order. Make sure to add the oil slowly.

Once the mayo is made, combine all the coleslaw ingredients in a large bowl with 1 cup (240 g) of the mayo. You can store the rest of the mayo for up to 2 weeks in the fridge. If you are preparing the slaw for a picnic or tailgate party, just combine it all in a zip-top bag. This slaw is best made in advance before serving.

BOOZY BOURBON SWEET POTATOES

I have served these sweet taters for years on the holidays. They became famous when I made a version of them with my bison tenderloin on *American Grilled*. I don't care for canned sweet potatoes. They are soggy mush. Raw sweet potatoes are easy to prepare and are so much more flavorful. The addition of the bourbon gives the potatoes a caramel flavor. The alcohol cooks out, so there is no need to worry about getting tipsy. That is, unless you enjoy a shot or two while they bake. Using wood to add smoke to the grill would pair perfectly with the bourbon.

SERVES: 4–6

3 large sweet potatoes

⅓ cup (50 g) raisins

¼ cup (38 g) chopped pecans

½ cup (112 g) unsalted butter, melted

1 cup (225 g) packed brown sugar

¼ cup (60 ml) bourbon

1 tsp (2 g) pumpkin pie spice

1 tsp (5 ml) pure vanilla extract

2 cups (100 g) mini marshmallows

Prepare your grill for two-zone cooking. If you are using a charcoal grill, burn the charcoal on only one side of your grill. If you have a gas grill, only light one side of your burners. Preheat the grill to 300°F (150°C). Grease a 9 x 9-inch (23 x 23-cm) baking dish.

Wrap the sweet potatoes in foil and grill them over indirect heat for 45 minutes, or until a fork will go through the potato with little resistance. The time will depend on the size of your tater. Remove them from the grill and peel off the skin: it should come right off. Slice the potatoes and layer them in the prepared baking dish. Sprinkle the raisins and pecans over the top.

In a small microwave-safe bowl, combine the butter, brown sugar, bourbon, pumpkin pie spice and vanilla. Heat the mixture in the microwave to dissolve the brown sugar most of the way. Pour the bourbon syrup over the sweet potatoes. Return the potatoes to the grill for 30 minutes, or until the bourbon mixture is thickened and bubbly. Spread the marshmallows over the potatoes and grill for 5 minutes more, until melted.

SWEET CORNBREAD

This is the moistest cornbread recipe I have ever had! I found it a couple of years ago and fell in love at first bite. The secret is the addition of honey to the batter. It adds flavor and another sweetness profile. I'm sure you could doctor it up with herbs or add corn to it. But why mess with something that ain't broke?

SERVES: 8–10

---

1 cup (140 g) cornmeal

3 cups (360 g) all-purpose flour

1⅓ cups (270 g) sugar

2 tbsp (16 g) baking powder

1 tsp (6 g) salt

⅔ cup (160 ml) vegetable oil

⅓ cup (75 g) butter, melted

2 tbsp (40 g) honey

4 eggs, beaten

2½ cups (590 ml) whole milk

Prepare your grill for two-zone cooking. If you are using a charcoal grill, burn the charcoal on only one side of your grill. If you have a gas grill, only light one side of your burners. Preheat the grill to 350°F (180°C) and grease a 9 x 13-inch (23 x 33-cm) baking dish.

Combine all the ingredients in a large bowl and stir just to moisten. Pour the batter into the prepared baking dish, place on the grill over indirect heat and cook for 45 minutes, or until it starts to brown and show cracks. This recipe can also be prepared in muffin pans. Grease or line the pans and adjust the cooking time to 20 to 25 minutes.

CHEESE POTATOES

These are the potatoes my mom makes for the holidays. There is nothing better than waking up to the smell of cheese taters and pork chops. That used to wake me up faster than any alarm clock. I made a couple of small changes to the original recipe . . . don't be mad, Mom. The cream of chicken soup is the secret ingredient here. It helps thicken the mix and adds a flavor that enhances the dish without screaming that it's chicken soup. These are better after they cool and thicken. For this dish, play with your smoking woods. Different woods add different flavors.

SERVES: 6–8

2 lb (908 g) russet potatoes

½ cup (80 g) diced yellow onion

1 tsp (6 g) salt

1 (10.5-oz [263-g]) can Campbell's Cream of Chicken soup

2 cloves roasted garlic (see Note, page 18)

1 lb (454 g) Velveeta cheese

2 cups (470 ml) milk

1 tbsp (14 g) unsalted butter

2 cups (240 g) shredded Kraft Triple Cheddar Cheese

Preheat the smoker to 275°F (135°C) and grease a 9 x 13-inch (23 x 33-cm) baking dish.

Peel and cut the potatoes into chunks. Add the potatoes to a large stockpot along with the onion and cover with water. Bring to boil, add the salt to the water and turn the heat down to a simmer. Cook the potatoes for 15 to 20 minutes, or until a fork can go through the potatoes easily. Drain the water from the pot and add the soup, garlic, Velveeta, milk and butter. Cover the pot with a lid and turn the heat down to low. Stir the potatoes after the cheese melts. If it's too thick, you can add a little bit more milk.

Pour into the prepared baking dish and top with the shredded cheese. Place the dish in the smoker and cook until the cheese is melted and bubbly, about 25 minutes.

SOUTHERN LIQUID REFRESHMENT AND TREATS FOR YOUR SWEET TOOTH

"AT HOME I SERVE THE KIND OF FOOD THAT I KNOW EVERY STORY BEHIND."

—MICHAEL POLLAN

I have always said the kitchen is the heart of the home. We gather there, we eat there and we create more there than food—we create memories. That seems to be the running theme with most of the book, and this chapter is no different. I hope you have enjoyed reading through the pages. I hope you have found one or two new recipes you want to try. Here are a few down-home sips and treats that complete any well-rounded meal.

GRILLED LEMONADE

Everyone is crazy about lemonade during the summer months, and most people enjoy a good cookout. Grilling anything makes it better in my book: the char, the intensity of flavor. That's what grilling does for lemons as well. The secret is that the heat caramelizes the natural sugars and releases the oils out of the lemon rind. The lemonade can be made Shirley Temple style or turned into an adult beverage by adding bourbon.

SERVES: 4–6

---

8 lemons, halved

Sugar, for sprinkling

SIMPLE SYRUP

1 cup (235 ml) water

1 cup (200 g) sugar

4 cups (940 ml) cold water

Ice cubes

Jim Beam Devil's Cut Bourbon, 1 shot per glass (optional)

Preheat your grill (unless it's already lit) to 300°F (150°C).

Sprinkle the cut lemons with some sugar. Place the lemons, cut side down, over the heat for 2 to 3 minutes, depending on how hot your fire is. Remove the lemons and allow them to cool. Juice the lemons with a handheld juicer into a pitcher. Add a couple of the lemon halves to the pitcher to infuse more flavor as it sits.

To make the simple syrup, heat the water and sugar in a saucepan over medium heat until the sugar is completely dissolved. Remove it from the heat and allow it to cool completely before adding it to the pitcher containing the lemon juice. Add the cold water and stir. Fill the pitcher up the rest of the way with ice. If desired, add a shot of bourbon to adult beverages.

PINEAPPLE ICED TEA

Sweet tea is a staple of the South and Southern cooking. There is nothing better than sitting on the front porch with a cold glass of sweet tea and watching the neighbors cruise by on their Sunday drive. This tea is sweetened with pineapple juice. If you like your tea a bit sweeter, just add more sugar. The secret to this tea is to grill the pineapple, which is full of natural sugars that become caramelized from the heat. By combining the caramelized pineapple and the bourbon you get a smoky sweet oak flavor.

SERVES: 6–8

4 cups (940 ml) water

7 Luzianne cold brew black tea bags

1 cup (235 ml) Dole pineapple juice

⅓ cup (80 ml) bourbon

2 tbsp (20 g) sugar

8 slices fresh pineapple

Ice

Preheat the grill to 300°F (150°C).

In a large saucepan, bring the water to a boil over high heat. Turn off the heat, add the tea bags and steep for 5 minutes. Discard the tea bags and stir in the pineapple juice, bourbon and sugar.

Grill the pineapple slices for 3 to 4 minutes on each side, or until you have good grill marks. Add the pineapple to the pitcher with the tea. Refrigerate for 2 hours to further develop the flavors. Serve over ice.

PEACH COBBLER MOONSHINE

A good cookbook from a Kentucky girl would not be complete without a moonshine recipe. There was an awful lot of white lightning made in the holler in front of my house by a neighbor who has since passed. My grandma and I would sit on the front porch all of the time. Didn't matter what time of day or night. One summer night we were on the porch and the smell blew up from the holler and about choked us to death. We had to get up and go in. I asked what that was and she said, "Oh, the neighbor is down there making moonshine again!" This may not be the real McCoy, but that doesn't stop it from being mighty tasty. The secret to bringing out the best flavor is to use fresh peaches.

SERVES: 8–10

4 ripe peaches, peeled, pitted and quartered

2 qt (1880 ml) white grape peach juice

1 (11.3-oz [316-g]) can peach nectar

1 cup (225 g) packed brown sugar

3–4 cinnamon sticks

1½ cups (355 ml) Everclear

½ cup (120 ml) peach schnapps

Preheat your grill to 300°F (150°C).

Grill the peaches, cut sides down, until they are golden and have good marks, about 5 minutes.

Combine the juices, sugar, peaches and cinnamon sticks in a large stockpot. Bring the juice to a simmer over medium heat and stir until the sugar has dissolved. Remove the pot from the heat and allow it to come to room temperature. After the mixture is cool, add the Everclear and schnapps. Pour the liquid into mason jars, seal and refrigerate until ready to serve.

PINEAPPLE UPSIDE-DOWN CAKE COCKTAIL

Sometimes I prefer to drink my dessert. This recipe tastes just like the real thing. The secret to the drink is to grill the pineapple to impart that "baked" flavor.

SERVES: 1

1 pineapple slice

1 oz (30 ml) cake- or vanilla-flavored vodka

1 oz (30 ml) pineapple juice

Splash of grenadine

1 maraschino cherry

Preheat the grill to 300°F (150°C).

Grill the pineapple slice until it is soft and has good grill marks, 3 to 4 minutes. Cut it in half. In a large shot glass, combine the vodka and pineapple juice. Place half of the pineapple slice in the bottom of the glass. Add the splash of grenadine and garnish with the other half of the pineapple and the cherry.

SPICY SMOKY GRAPEFRUIT MARGARITA

I am a huge fan of heat and spice and, combined with smoke, they are a delight to the senses. The secret is the addition of honey to sweeten the drink. It highlights the smoke flavor to create a very unique, refreshing cocktail.

SERVES: 4

2 grapefruits

2 limes

1 cup (235 ml) tequila

½ cup (120 ml) orange liqueur

2 cups (470 ml) grapefruit juice

¾ cup (180 ml) fresh lime juice

4 tbsp (80 g) honey, plus more for rimming the glasses

2 grilled jalapeños, sliced

Kosher salt, for rimming the glasses

Ice

Preheat your grill to 300°F (150°C).

Cut the grapefruits and limes in half and place on the grill to add char and grill marks, about 4 minutes on each side. Remove from the grill and reserve 2 lime slices and 2 grapefruit slices to use as garnish. Cut the slices in half.

Place the remaining slices in a pitcher and add the tequila, orange liqueur, grapefruit juice, lime juice, honey and most of the sliced jalapeños, reserving 4 for garnish. Stir to blend and place in the refrigerator for 30 minutes or up to 2 hours depending on the spice level you prefer.

When you are ready to serve, drizzle some honey onto a shallow plate and spread the kosher salt on another plate. Dip the rim of each glass into the honey, then into the salt. Add ice to each glass and strain the margarita into the glasses. Garnish with the reserved lime and grapefruit halves and a jalapeño slice.

STRAWBERRY KEY LIME SLUSH

Most drinks are made from regular limes. The secret to this refreshing drink is the use of grilled Key limes, which are smaller and a bit more tart than regular limes. If you want to serve this cocktail as a dessert, top off each glass with a scoop of vanilla ice cream.

SERVES: 2

About 1 lb (908 g) Key limes or ½–⅔ cup (118–160 ml) Key lime juice

2 cups (470 ml) water

1 cup (200 g) sugar

2 cups (290 g) fresh strawberries, hulled

3 cups (300 g) ice

3 oz (90 ml) Cîroc vodka

Preheat the grill to 300°F (150°C).

Cut the Key limes in half and place them, cut side down, on the grill. Grill the limes for 5 minutes, or until caramelized. Remove them from the heat and use a juicer to juice the limes. You need 1 cup (235 ml). Next, in a saucepan bring the water to a boil and add the sugar. Remove the pan from the heat and stir until the sugar is dissolved. Set the sugar water in the fridge to cool. In a blender, combine the strawberries, ice, Key lime juice, vodka and cooled sugar water. Blend until smooth.

WATERGATE SALAD

Can you throw together a tasty dessert in less than 5 minutes? This is one I grew up with for holidays and it's the other sweet my son asks for on "the feast." A simple oldie but goodie. The secret is the pistachio pudding. It adds flavor and also thickens the dessert.

SERVES: 10

1 (20-oz [560-g]) can sliced pineapple

1 (3.4-oz [95-g]) package Jell-O pistachio instant pudding mix

1 (10.5-oz [294-g]) bag mini marshmallows

1 (8-oz [227-g]) container Cool Whip, thawed

½ cup (75 g) chopped pecans

Light your grill to medium-high heat (300°F [150°C]). Place the pineapple slices on the grill over direct heat and grill on each side for 3 minutes. Remove the pineapple from the grill and chill. Finely chop the pineapple and combine with the rest of the ingredients.

GRILLED STRAWBERRY PIE

I love using fresh strawberries and strawberry gel to make a simple strawberry pie in the summer. But when the weather cools and I crave something warm and soul soothing, I break out my grilled strawberry pie recipe. The secret to the perfect glaze is strawberry preserves. I use preserves that I canned at home, but a good store-bought variety will work just fine.

SERVES: 6

3 cups (435 g) fresh strawberries, hulled and sliced

¼ cup (50 g) sugar

1 tbsp (8 g) cornstarch

¼ cup (60 g) strawberry preserves

1 store-bought pie crust

Prepare your grill for two-zone cooking. If you are using a charcoal grill, burn the charcoal on only one side of your grill. If you have a gas grill, only light one side of your burners. Preheat your grill to 375°F (190°C).

In a bowl, combine the strawberries, sugar, cornstarch and preserves and stir to coat the strawberries well. Unroll the pie crust onto a cookie sheet. Place the strawberry filling into the center of the crust and fold the edges of crust over the filling, creating a rustic galette. Place the pie on the grill over indirect heat and grill until the crust is golden and the filling is bubbly, 25 to 30 minutes.

APPLE PIE GRILLED DOUGHNUTS

I love warm, fresh doughnuts! It is super easy to make your own at home with the grill instead of a deep fryer. The secret is using good-quality biscuits and brushing them with melted butter in order to get the seasoned sugar to stick. You can serve these babies with ice cream, fruit, whipped cream, you name it. There is not one thing that I'm afraid to put on a grill! If you add applewood to the fire, it will accentuate the apple pie seasoning.

SERVES: 8

1 (16.3-oz [462-g]) can Grands! Southern Homestyle Buttermilk Biscuits

4 tbsp (56 g) unsalted butter, melted

¼ cup (50 g) granulated sugar

2 tbsp (30 g) packed light brown sugar

1 tsp (2 g) apple pie spice

Preheat your grill to 225°F (100°C).

Remove the biscuits from the can and cut out the center using a small round spice lid or a knife. Place the doughnuts and holes over the heat and grill for 4 to 6 minutes per side. Remove them from the heat and brush the melted butter all over the doughnuts. Combine the sugars and spice in a bowl and roll the doughnuts in the mixture to coat.

CHOCOLATE CHIP COOKIE BACON S'MORES

The best part about cooking outside and sitting around a fire is making s'mores. Yes, I am a kid at heart and will never grow up. But, as a chef and an adult I started to wonder, what could top that gooey, chocolaty goodness? The secret? BACON! Everything is better with bacon. The soft cookie is a terrific boat to contain all the heaping flavors in the middle. This is very much an insane adult version of that childhood favorite.

SERVES: 12

1 (1-lb [454-g]) package refrigerated chocolate chip cookie dough (to make 24 cookies)

12 slices bacon

2 (1.55-oz [43-g]) Hershey's chocolate bars or your favorite chocolate

12 large marshmallows

Preheat your grill to 300°F (150°C).

Bake the cookies according to package directions and let them cool for at least 10 minutes so they will not be too soft. Place the bacon on the grill and grill for 8 to 10 minutes, turning halfway through. Remove the bacon from the grill and set aside. For each s'more, place one cookie upside down and place 2 squares of chocolate on the cookie. Next, grill your marshmallows on skewers until your desired doneness and place it on the chocolate. Top the marshmallow with a folded slice of bacon and another cookie on top. Oh-so-messy and oh-so-sinful.

ACKNOWLEDGMENTS

Thank you, Mom, for always being there when I needed you, for listening and helping me every step of the way and for watching my babies when I had a competition.

Thank you, Dad, for watching over me and passing on to me my passion for grilling, my competitive character and my love of nature and hunting.

Thank you, Grandma, for starting my love affair with food and all things food-related, and for watching over me and keeping me safe.

Thank you, Andrew, for seeing these things in me even before those stars were within my reach. You sure called it.

I must thank Page Street Publishing for taking a chance on this country girl and believing in my ability. I hope I make you proud.

Thanks to Ken Goodman for taking the time to put up with me and shooting the beautiful photos for my book.

Thank you, Danny, for keeping me together and on-track, for the prep and cooking for the photos. I wouldn't trust anyone else to handle these recipes. You have been the glue for sure.

Thank you to the cities of Maysville, Kentucky and Washington, Kentucky for allowing us the use of Mefford's Fort.

And thank you to my barbecue family for sharing the love and friendship.

ABOUT THE AUTHOR

Staci Graves Jett is a competitive cook, a chef, a butcher and an author. She competed in 2014 on the Travel Channel's *American Grilled*, where she won the title of Louisville Grillmaster and $10,000. In 2015, she competed on the Food Network's *Chopped Grill Masters*. Staci has also competed at Memphis in May. She has many awards under her hat, including a perfect 180 at the Tryon, North Carolina barbecue competition and spots at the World Food Championships.

INDEX